# Table of Contents

# Introduction

The goal of this book is to improve students' reading and comprehension skills. The more experience a child has with reading and comprehending, the better reader and problem solver he or she will be. *Daily Warm-Ups: Reading* contains a variety of passages to be read on a daily basis. Each passage is followed by comprehension questions. The questions that follow the passages are based on Bloom's Taxonomy and allow for higher–level thinking skills. Making this book a part of your daily classroom agenda can help your students' reading and comprehension abilities improve dramatically.

## Nonfiction and Fiction

*Daily Warm-Ups: Reading* is divided into two sections: nonfiction and fiction. It is important for students to be exposed to a variety of reading genres and formats. The nonfiction section is divided into five categories. These categories are animals, biography, American history, science, and current events. By reading these nonfiction passages, your students will be exposed to a variety of nonfiction information, as well as questions to stimulate thinking on these subjects.

The fiction section of the book is also divided into five categories. These categories are fairy tales/folklore, historical fiction, contemporary realistic fiction, mystery/suspense/adventure, and fantasy. Each story is followed by questions to stimulate thinking about the plot, characters, vocabulary, and sequence.

## Comprehension Questions

Comprehension is the primary goal of any reading task. Students who comprehend what they read perform better both on tests and in life. The follow-up questions after each passage are written to encourage students to improve in recognizing text structure, visualizing, summarizing, and learning new vocabulary. Each of these skills can be found in scope-and-sequence charts as well as standards for reading comprehension. The different types of questions in *Daily Warm-Ups: Reading* are geared to help students with the following skills:

- Recognize the main idea
- Identify details
- Recall details
- Summarize
- Describe characters and character traits
- Classify and sort into categories
- Compare and contrast

- Make generalizations
- Draw conclusions
- Recognize fact
- Apply information to new situations
- Recognize sequence
- Understand vocabulary

## Readability

Each of the reading passages in *Daily Warm-Ups: Reading* varies in difficulty to meet the various reading levels of your students. The passages have been categorized as follows: below grade level, at grade level, and above grade level. (See Leveling Chart on page 175.)

## Record Keeping

Use the tracking sheet on page 6 to record which warm-up exercises you have given to your students. Or, distribute copies of the sheet for students to keep their own records. Use the certificate on page 176 as you see fit. You can use the certificate as a reward for students completing a certain number of warm-up exercises. Or, you may choose to distribute the certificates to students who complete the warm-up exercises with 100% accuracy.

## How to Make the Most of This Book

Here are some simple tips, which you may have already thought of, already implemented, or may be new to you. They are only suggestions to help you make your students as successful in reading as possible.

- Read through the book ahead of time so you are familiar with each portion. The better you understand how the book works, the easier it will be to answer students' questions.

- Set aside a regular time each day to incorporate *Daily Warm-Ups* into your routine. Once the routine is established, students will look forward to and expect to work on reading strategies at that particular time.

- Make sure that any amount of time spent on *Daily Warm-Ups* is positive and constructive. This should be a time of practicing for success and recognizing it as it is achieved.

- Allot only about 10 minutes to *Daily Warm-Ups*. Too much time will not be useful; too little time will create additional stress.

- Be sure to model the reading and question-answering process at the beginning of the year. Model pre-reading questions, reading the passage, highlighting information that refers to the questions, and eliminating answers that are obviously wrong. Finally, refer back to the text once again, to make sure the answers chosen are the best ones.

- Create and store overheads of each lesson so that you can review student work, concepts, and strategies as quickly as possible.

- Utilize peer tutors who have strong skills for peer interaction to assist with struggling students.

- Offer small group time to students who need extra enrichment or opportunities for questions regarding the text. Small groups will allow many of these students, once they are comfortable with the format, to achieve success independently.

- Adjust the procedures, as you see fit, to meet the needs of all your students.

# Tracking Sheet

## NONFICTION

| Animals | | Biography | | American History | | Science | | Currents Events | |
|---|---|---|---|---|---|---|---|---|---|
| Page 9 | | Page 25 | | Page 41 | | Page 56 | | Page 72 | |
| Page 10 | | Page 26 | | Page 42 | | Page 57 | | Page 73 | |
| Page 11 | | Page 27 | | Page 43 | | Page 58 | | Page 74 | |
| Page 12 | | Page 28 | | Page 44 | | Page 59 | | Page 75 | |
| Page 13 | | Page 29 | | Page 45 | | Page 60 | | Page 76 | |
| Page 14 | | Page 30 | | Page 46 | | Page 61 | | Page 77 | |
| Page 15 | | Page 31 | | Page 47 | | Page 62 | | Page 78 | |
| Page 16 | | Page 32 | | Page 48 | | Page 63 | | Page 79 | |
| Page 17 | | Page 33 | | Page 49 | | Page 64 | | Page 80 | |
| Page 18 | | Page 34 | | Page 50 | | Page 65 | | Page 81 | |
| Page 19 | | Page 35 | | Page 51 | | Page 66 | | Page 82 | |
| Page 20 | | Page 36 | | Page 52 | | Page 67 | | Page 83 | |
| Page 21 | | Page 37 | | Page 53 | | Page 68 | | Page 84 | |
| Page 22 | | Page 38 | | Page 54 | | Page 69 | | Page 85 | |
| Page 23 | | Page 39 | | Page 55 | | Page 70 | | Page 86 | |
| Page 24 | | Page 40 | | | | Page 71 | | | |

## FICTION

| Fairy Tales/ Folklore | | Historical Fiction | | Contemporary Realistic Fiction | | Mystery/Suspense/ Adventure | | Fantasy | |
|---|---|---|---|---|---|---|---|---|---|
| Page 89 | | Page 105 | | Page 120 | | Page 136 | | Page 152 | |
| Page 90 | | Page 106 | | Page 121 | | Page 137 | | Page 153 | |
| Page 91 | | Page 107 | | Page 122 | | Page 138 | | Page 154 | |
| Page 92 | | Page 108 | | Page 123 | | Page 139 | | Page 155 | |
| Page 93 | | Page 109 | | Page 124 | | Page 140 | | Page 156 | |
| Page 94 | | Page 110 | | Page 125 | | Page 141 | | Page 157 | |
| Page 95 | | Page 111 | | Page 126 | | Page 142 | | Page 158 | |
| Page 96 | | Page 112 | | Page 127 | | Page 143 | | Page 159 | |
| Page 97 | | Page 118 | | Page 128 | | Page 144 | | Page 160 | |
| Page 98 | | Page 114 | | Page 129 | | Page 145 | | Page 161 | |
| Page 99 | | Page 115 | | Page 130 | | Page 146 | | Page 162 | |
| Page 100 | | Page 116 | | Page 131 | | Page 147 | | Page 163 | |
| Page 101 | | Page 117 | | Page 132 | | Page 148 | | Page 164 | |
| Page 102 | | Page 118 | | Page 133 | | Page 149 | | Page 165 | |
| Page 103 | | Page 119 | | Page 134 | | Page 150 | | Page 166 | |
| Page 104 | | | | Page 135 | | Page 151 | | | |

# NONFICTION

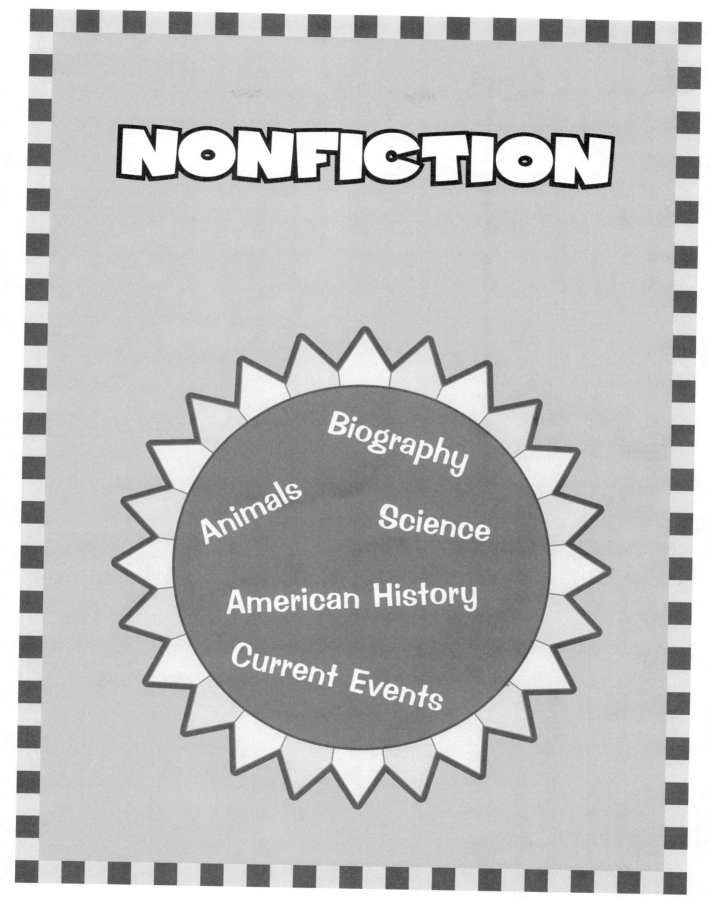

8

Name _____    Date _____

# LADYBUGS

Have you ever seen a small, red beetle with black dots on its back?  These little insects are called ladybugs.  These little insects are harmless to humans.  A ladybug does not bite or sting humans.  Ladybugs are also harmless to plants, and they do not carry diseases.  But how did the ladybug get its name?  There are many stories.  One of these stories came from the Middle Ages.  The crops were being eaten, and the villagers began praying.  The red beetles with black dots came and ate the harmful insects.  These beetles were named "the Beetles of Our Lady."  The name was shortened to lady beetles or ladybugs.

Since then, the ladybug has been known to bring good luck.  There are many beliefs about ladybugs from all over the world.  It has been said that if a ladybug lands on a young maiden's hand, she will marry soon.  In England, it has been said that if a farmer sees a ladybug, he will have a good harvest.  Some people believe that the number of spots you see on the ladybug's back will represent the number of children you will have.

Ladybugs today can still bring good fortune.  If you have a ladybug in your garden, then you do not need to use insect poison to get rid of aphids.  Aphids are tiny insects that are harmful to many plants.  They suck the juice from the leaves of the plant.  A ladybug can eat as many as 50 aphids in a day.  Some people buy ladybugs to fight the aphids.

## STORY QUESTIONS

1. According to this reading passage, why might someone want to buy a ladybug?
   a. They are more expensive than insecticides.
   b. Ladybugs kill aphids that can be harmful to plants.
   c. Ladybugs bring good luck.
   d. Ladybugs will reproduce.

2. This passage is mostly about . . .
   a. aphids.
   b. good farming practices.
   c. the anatomy of a ladybug.
   d. general information of ladybugs.

3. According to the passage, what do some people believe will happen when a ladybug lands on the hand of a young maiden?

   _____

   _____

4. According to the passage, what might ladybugs first have been called?
   a. lady in waiting
   b. lady buggle
   c. the Beetles of Our Lady
   d. bug of a lady

Name _____  Date _____

# THE PANDA BEAR

One of the most unusual bears known to man is the panda bear. Panda bears live in southwestern China. They live in misty forests of bamboo. There are two main types of pandas. They are the giant black-and-white panda and the red panda. They weigh anywhere from 175 to 275 pounds. They get anywhere from five to six feet in height. A newborn panda cub is about the size of a chipmunk. They are born blind and are completely helpless. They rely heavily on their mother. Once the baby panda leaves its mother, it will live all alone.

Pandas are active during both the day and at night. The most important plant in the life of a panda bear is bamboo. They spend about 12 hours of their day eating bamboo. That's a lot of bamboo! Pandas have special bones in their wrists that enable them to grab the stalks of the bamboo. Pandas will peel away the outer edge of the stalk and eat the soft inner portion of the bamboo. Their giant molars crush the bamboo stalks. The panda will also eat the bamboo leaves. Pandas have also been known to eat mushrooms, insects, grasses, fish, fruit, and rice.

Pandas move in a very slow, methodical manner. Unlike some bears, the panda bear does not hibernate. They live in a climate where they can be active and eating throughout the year.

## STORY QUESTIONS

**1.** A different title for this reading passage could be . . .
   a. "Panda Paradise."          c. "All You Want to Know About Bears."
   b. "China's Bear."            d. "Illegal Bear Hunting."

**2.** Newborn panda cubs are <u>not</u> born . . .
   a. being able to see.          c. the size of a chipmunk.
   b. blind.                  d. helpless.

**3.** The author wrote this passage to . . .
   a. justify keeping pandas in captivity.
   b. inform the reader of how pandas are mistreated.
   c. share general information about panda bears.
   d. raise awareness of the shrinking of the panda population.

**4.** If you wanted to find out more about pandas, you could . . .
   a. read a book about how bears hibernate.
   b. watch a television program about bamboo.
   c. meet somebody who lives in China.
   d. watch a television program about the different types of bears.

# KILLER WHALES

Have you ever heard of the killer whale? Did you know that killer whales live in oceans all over the world? They are found mostly in the Arctic and Antarctic oceans, where the water is cold. Killer whales can also be spotted on both shores of the United States. Killer whales have been spotted in warmer waters such as the Bahamas and the Gulf of Mexico. This just goes to show how adaptable the killer whale can be.

How do killer whales differ from other whales? One way is in their coloring. A killer whale is striking in its coloring of black and white. This makes it easy to spot. Killer whales have a sleek body form. They are smaller when compared to most whales. Killer whales are typically 19–22 feet long and can weigh anywhere from 8,000 to 12,000 pounds.

Killer whales get their name for a reason. They are the top predators in the ocean. Killer whales will eat almost any kind of sea animal including sea lions, fish, squid, seals, walruses, birds, sea turtles, penguins, and otters. It's been recorded that even a moose has been found in the stomach of a killer whale. Killer whales are very agile and can move quickly through the water. In fact, they are the fastest swimming marine mammals. This speed and agility makes it easy for the killer whale to hunt. Often times, killer whales will hunt in groups. This improves their chances of catching prey.

## STORY QUESTIONS

1. What is this passage mainly about?
   a. how the killer whale eats
   b. predators of the killer whale
   c. the different types of whales
   d. general facts about the killer whale

2. In the last paragraph, what does the word *recorded* mean?
   a. tape recorded
   b. documented
   c. measured
   d. opened

3. To improve their chances of catching prey, killer whales often . . .
   a. hunt animals that can't swim.
   b. hunt tiny animals.
   c. hunt in groups.
   d. attack at sunset.

4. Based on information in the passage, how did the killer whale get its name?
   a. by hunting in groups
   b. by being black and white
   c. by being smaller than most whales
   d. by being the top predator of the ocean

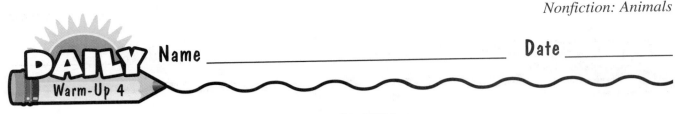

Name _____     Date _____

# THE SLOTH

What is a sloth?  Did you know that a sloth is a slow-moving animal that lives in trees?  Sometimes people are called sloths, but that's not because they live in trees; rather, it's because they are moving so slowly.  A sloth spends most of its time hanging upside down in a tree.  A sloth will eat, sleep, and give birth hanging upside down!  Their curved claws make it easy for them to hang onto the tree.

Sloths are four-legged animals.  They spend almost all of their lives up in a tree.  They walk upside down along the branches.  Sloths are also known to be good swimmers.  Sloths are found in Central and South America.

The sloth is nocturnal, which means it is active at night instead of the day.  This means that it sleeps during the day.  The sloth usually keeps to itself, although some female sloths congregate in small groups.

The sloth has a thick, brown coat of fur.  They are plant-eaters and eat mostly leaves, tender shoots, and fruit.  The sloth has green algae growing on its fur.  The sloth will lick the algae for nutrients.  The algae also helps protect the sloth from enemies.  Eagles, jaguars, and humans hunt the sloth.  The algae growing on the sloth helps to camouflage it.

## STORY QUESTIONS

1. In order for a sloth to live in a tree, it needs . . .
   a. courage.
   b. to be the right size.
   c. curved claws.
   d. to eat only plants.

2. According to the passage, how do sloths keep from being eaten?
   a. They are easily hidden.
   b. They are camouflaged by green algae.
   c. They are slow moving.
   d. They have thick, brown fur.

3. Why did the author include the first paragraph?
   a. to introduce the main points about the sloth
   b. to clear up misconceptions about the sloth
   c. to generate questions about the sloth
   d. to identify the food eaten by the sloth

4. The best way to find the answer to question #3 above is to . . .
   a. reread the entire passage.
   b. reread the first paragraph and determine the main idea.
   c. look for the words "sloth" and "habitat."
   d. skim the passage and look for clues.

**Name** _____  **Date** _____

# THE RATTLESNAKE

Have you ever heard the rattle of a rattlesnake? In the wild, it can be one of the scariest sounds around. The rattlesnake is venomous, which means it is poisonous. A rattlesnake has something that sounds like a rattle at the end of its body. The rattle is an organ made up of loosely-attached pieces of horn. When rattled, the pieces of horn bounce against each other, making the rattle sound. The body of a rattlesnake is grayish or brownish gray with darker circular blotches along its back and sides. The underside of the rattlesnake is a creamish color.

The rattle on a rattlesnake is used to warn an intruder that the snake is there. A rattlesnake usually bites a person when someone tries to catch, kill, or harm it. When a rattlesnake bites a person, he or she should be treated with anti-venom, which fights the poison in the body. Most people do not die when a rattlesnake has bitten them. But when people are bitten by a rattlesnake, they should receive immediate medical attention.

What does a rattlesnake eat? A rattlesnake doesn't want to eat a human when and if it bites one; it is only trying to defend itself. Rattlesnakes eat rodents. This helps control the rodent population. Rattlesnakes need rodents and a place to hide in order to survive. Rattlesnakes stay in the same general area, but they will not fight other rattlesnakes.

## STORY QUESTIONS

**1.** How does the author feel about rattlesnakes?
   a. The author is in favor of rattlesnake control.
   b. The author has been bitten by a rattlesnake and dislikes them.
   c. The author is afraid of rattlesnakes.
   d. The author sees the need and purpose for rattlesnakes.

**2.** The second paragraph instructs readers on what . . .
   a. to do if they see a rattlesnake.        c. a rattlesnake looks like.
   b. to do if bitten by a rattlesnake.        d. a rattlesnakes preys on.

**3.** Will a rattlesnake eat a human?
   a. Yes, if they are threatened by one.      c. No, they eat rodents.
   b. No, unless they are starving.            d. Yes, when there are no rodents around.

**4.** Where might this information about the rattlesnake most likely be found?
   a. in a pamphlet on rattlesnakes
   b. on a cereal box
   c. in a book about rodents
   d. in a book about the Northwest

# THE PRAYING MANTIS

The praying mantis has one of the most unusual names for an insect. How did this insect get its name? The praying mantis got its name because of the way it sits and waits for its prey. The way that the praying mantis sits makes it look like it is praying. Did you know that the praying mantis is related to the cockroach?

The praying mantis is a meat-eating insect. It eats beetles, butterflies, crickets, grasshoppers, spiders, and even other praying mantises. An adult praying mantis can sometimes eat small reptiles or small hummingbirds! A praying mantis is green or tan, and its back makes it look like a leaf. This means that it is easy for the praying mantis to be camouflaged. A praying mantis also has wings. The adult is usually 3–6 inches long. Some species can get even longer.

The praying mantis is a very quick predator. It waits for the right size bug to come along and snaps its "arms" out quickly. The claws on the "arms" make it impossible for the insect to escape the praying mantis. Bats eat praying mantises. The praying mantis tends to fly more at night. This makes it a perfect target for bats.

## STORY QUESTIONS

1. Where in the passage do you find out which insect the praying mantis is related to?
   a. end of the first paragraph
   b. middle of the second paragraph
   c. end of the third paragraph
   d. from the title

2. What does the praying mantis have that helps the bat spot it at night?
   a. claw-like arms
   b. wings
   c. eggs
   d. strong scent

3. The writer probably wrote this passage to . . .
   a. warn humans of the praying mantis.
   b. enlighten farmers to the benefits of the praying mantis.
   c. determine the genealogy of the praying mantis.
   d. inform the reader about the praying mantis.

4. Which of these is not a fact about the praying mantis?
   a. The praying mantis is a meat-eating insect.
   b. The praying mantis catches its prey.
   c. The praying mantis is red in color.
   d. The praying mantis is about 3–6 inches long.

Name _____

Date _____

# THE BISON

One of the most hunted animals of all time is the bison. The bison, also known as the buffalo, used to number between 30 and 60 million. Today there are only about 200,000 bison remaining. Only 16,000 of these are wild bison. The wild, free-roaming bison are located at Yellowstone National Park. People used to kill the bison for their thick, furry hides. Bison almost became extinct in 1890. Efforts were then made to try and save the bison.

The bison eat grasses and sedges. *Sedge* is a type of plant. Bison are known to keep moving as they graze on the grasses. This keeps any area from being overgrazed. The bison is a big animal. In fact, it is the heaviest land mammal in North America. The bison can get as big as 2,200 pounds. It stands anywhere from 5 to 6 ½ feet tall.

Bison are social animals that live in herds of about 20–50. The females lead the herd. The bulls (males) live alone or in small groups. The bison can reach speeds as fast as 35 miles per hour. Look out!

## STORY QUESTIONS

1. Ranchers and farmers would probably like to have bison graze on their land because . . .
   a. bison are shy and feisty animals.
   b. can reach speeds up to 35 mph.
   c. bison keep moving as they eat, which prevents overgrazing.
   d. bison live in herds or small groups.

2. According to the passage, what efforts do you think were made to prevent the extinction of the bison?
   a. bison were let free and allowed to roam wild
   b. laws were passed and rules made about the killing of bison
   c. the president made it illegal to shoot a bison
   d. bison live in herds or small groups

3. What is the main idea of the passage?
   a. The bison can run very quickly.
   b. The bison is an extinct animal.
   c. The bison engage in social activity.
   d. The bison is an interesting animal and has an interesting history.

4. The bison is the heaviest land mammal in . . .
   a. North America.
   b. the Orient.
   c. South America.
   d. Central America.

**Name** _____ **Date** _____

DAILY Warm-Up 8

# FLAMINGOS

Can you imagine what a pink bird with long legs would look like? If so, you would be picturing a flamingo. In fact, a flamingo stands up to 51 inches tall, but only weighs approximately seven-and-a-half pounds. It takes about two years for a flamingo to reach its full height. The male flamingo stands taller than the female flamingo.

The bright pinkish color for which the flamingo is known doesn't come right away. Baby flamingos are born gray or white. It is said that the feathers of a flamingo turn pink because of the food they eat. The flamingo's legs are very long and spindly. What looks like the flamingo's knee is actually its ankle joint. The knee is located up closer to the body. The flamingo has webbing between its toes to aid in swimming and stirring up food.

So, what does the flamingo eat? Well, it's probably not something you will find on your dinner plate any time soon. The flamingo eats algae, insect larva, adult insects, crustaceans, and small fish. The shape of a flamingo's bill will determine the type of food it will eat. Flamingos have either a shallow or deep-keeled bill. The flamingos with shallow bills eat more of the fish and crustaceans. The ones with deep-keeled bills eat more of the algae. You might have seen a flamingo hang its head upside down in the water. The flamingo was probably eating. Yum!

## STORY QUESTIONS

1. What is the purpose of the webbing between the toes of the flamingo?
   a. to stabilize the flamingo from falling over
   b. a characteristic used to identify the difference between flamingo species
   c. to help the flamingo protect itself
   d. to aid the flamingo in swimming and gathering food

2. Identify a supporting detail that explains the statement, "The shape of a flamingo's bill will determine the type of food it will eat."
   a. Flamingos have either a shallow or deep-keeled bill.
   b. The flamingos with shallow bills eat more of the fish and crustaceans.
   c. The flamingo's legs are very long and spindly.
   d. The male flamingo stands taller than the female flamingo.

3. After reading the passage, which question could you answer about the flamingo?
   a. How does the flamingo protect itself?
   b. How many different types of flamingos are there?
   c. What is the best known reason as to how the flamingo gets the color in its feathers?
   d. How does the mother flamingo feed her young?

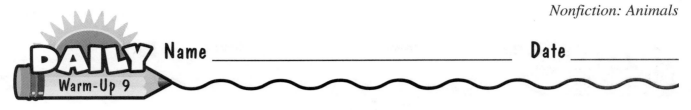

# THE GIRAFFE

Can you name the tallest mammal? If you said giraffe, you are correct. The male giraffe is taller than the female giraffe. Did you know that the male giraffe can get as tall as 19 feet? The female giraffe is still very tall. She gets as tall as 16 feet. The giraffe is a heavy mammal. A male giraffe can weigh between 2,000–3,000 pounds.

In the wild, the giraffe usually lives about 25 years. The giraffe lives mostly in Central, Eastern, and Southern Africa. A giraffe makes its home on the savannas of Africa. The savanna has tall trees, arid land, open plains, and forests. The giraffe eats leaves from the trees for nourishment. They usually eat the leaves of the acacia tree. A giraffe can go a very long time without drinking water. It is able to get moisture from the tree leaves.

The giraffe is a social animal, which means that it likes to live in groups with other giraffes, called herds. These herds can get very large and are not organized in any specific way. Because giraffes have such interesting coats, they are often hunted. They are also hunted for their meat and tails. The tails are made into good-luck bracelets. Unfortunately, there are no current laws protecting the giraffe.

## STORY QUESTIONS

1. Which sentence in the last paragraph shows how the author feels about hunting giraffes?
   a. Giraffes are hunted for their meat and tails.
   b. Unfortunately, there are no current laws protecting the giraffe.
   c. The giraffe has such an interesting coat.
   d. The tails are made into good luck bracelets.

2. According to this passage, giraffes are hunted for their . . .
   a. interesting coats and tails.
   b. great height.
   c. good luck.
   d. meat and teeth.

3. You can conclude that a giraffe would probably do well living in . . .
   a. the Sonoran Desert.
   b. mountain ranges.
   c. dry land with plenty of trees.
   d. the Everglades.

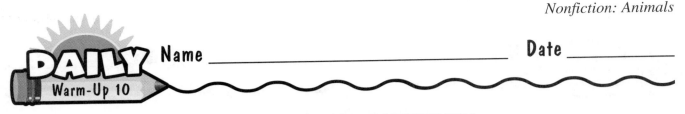

**DAILY**
Warm-Up 10

**Name** _____ **Date** _____

# THE MONARCH BUTTERFLY

Have you ever heard of a royal butterfly? That would be the monarch butterfly. The monarch butterfly gets its name from its beautiful color and regal look. The monarch butterfly is bright orange with black veins and white dots.

A butterfly is a type of insect. It has six legs, three body parts, wings, and a pair of eyes. The monarch butterfly goes through a long process to get to its final stage. Each butterfly begins as an egg. The larva hatches from the egg in about three to five days. The larvae are in the shape of a caterpillar. In this stage, the larva eats until it gets to be about two inches long, which takes about a week. It will then find a hidden branch. Here it forms into a pupa or a chrysalis. It takes between 10 and 12 days for the butterfly to form and emerge from its chrysalis. As an adult, the butterfly can only drink liquids.

It may surprise you to learn that the monarch butterfly is poisonous. Animals that eat the monarch get sick and vomit. These animals remember the brightly-colored butterfly and learn to avoid it. The nonpoisonous viceroy butterfly mimics the color of the monarch butterfly to avoid being eaten. Monarch butterflies are found in fields, marshes, meadows, and in the garden. You may have a monarch butterfly flying around your garden right now.

## STORY QUESTIONS

1. In this passage, the word *mimics* means?
   a. mocks
   b. imitates
   c. patronizes
   d. humiliates

2. Which statement is false?
   a. The monarch butterfly is poisonous.
   b. The monarch butterfly emerges from a chrysalis.
   c. The monarch butterfly mimics the viceroy butterfly.
   d. The larva hatches from the egg.

3. From start to finish, how long does it take for the monarch butterfly to go from an egg to a butterfly?
   a. two weeks
   b. 10 to 14 days
   c. six months
   d. about three weeks

# DESERT TORTOISE

The desert tortoise gets its name because it lives in the desert. This means that the tortoise has to adapt to live in an arid, hot climate. Its habitat can be found in Southern California, Nevada, Arizona, and in parts of Mexico. Just like turtles, the desert tortoise has a shell that is usually brown and tan in color and is very hard. The shell can be anywhere from 8–15 feet long. The tortoise's body is not designed to swim (like a turtle's body is).

You may wonder how the tortoise can survive the extreme heat. The desert tortoise can handle up to 140-degree temperatures by burrowing itself into the ground to escape the heat. The desert tortoise spends most of its life in a burrow. It makes a hissing or a popping sound when it is afraid.

The desert tortoise eats herbs, grasses, and the new growth of cacti. The flowers of the cactus are eaten as well. This animal is more active during the daytime—especially in the early morning and early evening. It can live to be 50–80 years old! That is old for an animal. The tortoise hatches its young from eggs. The temperature actually determines whether it will be a male or female tortoise. The desert tortoise is endangered. Let's do what we can to protect this interesting animal!

## STORY QUESTIONS

1. Compared to the turtle, the desert tortoise can . . .
   a. withstand extreme heat.
   b. swim in the water.
   c. grow a hard shell.
   d. hatch their young from eggs.

2. The word *cacti* is the plural form of . . .
   a. extreme temperature.
   b. caterpillar.
   c. cactus.
   d. cactus flowers.

3. Why do you think the shell is so important to the tortoise?
   a. It prevents it from getting wet.
   b. It helps the tortoise move quickly.
   c. It stores food.
   d. It serves as a protection.

4. A synonym for *arid* (which is found in the first paragraph) is . . .
   a. high in the sky.
   b. dry and parched.
   c. protected.
   d. endangered.

Name _____   Date _____

# CLOWN FISH

Did you know that a clown lives in the ocean?  That's right.  The clown fish lives in the ocean.  The clown fish gets its name because it looks like it has a clown face painted on to its face.  It's not really makeup or paint; it's just how the clown fish looks.  The well-known clown fish is colored bright orange and white.  There are other types of clown fish that come in different bright colors.

The coloring of the clown fish makes it easy for its enemy to spot it.  In order to stay safe, the clown fish hides inside the "branches" of the sea anemone.  The sea anemone looks like a small bush in the ocean.  The branches of the sea anemone are poisonous.  The tentacles can sting the fish.  You may wonder how the clown fish keeps from getting hurt.  The answer is that the clown fish is unaffected by the venom of the sea anemone.  It is the only fish like this.

What does the clown fish eat?  The clown fish eats zooplankton.  Zooplankton are very tiny animals that float around in the seawater.  Sometimes they are so small that you cannot see them without a microscope.

## STORY QUESTIONS

**1.** When do you think a clown fish would leave the sea anemone's tentacles?

   a. to seek food

   b. to seek safety

   c. to chase away its enemy

   d. to recover from the poison of the sea anemone

**2.** Which statement is true?

   a. The sea anemone is related to the clown fish.

   b. The clown fish must be careful to avoid the anemone's tentacles.

   c. Most of the animals that eat sea anemone eat clown fish as well.

   d. Clown fish are brightly-colored fish.

**3.** In this passage, the word *unaffected* means . . .

   a. unchanged.

   b. unharmed.

   c. killed instantly.

   d. unchallenged.

Name _____  Date _____

# THE MOUNTAIN LION

Just hearing the name of this animal brings fear to many people. The mountain lion has many names. You may recognize some of them, such as cougar, puma, and panther. The mountain lion is a magnificent hunter with grace and speed. Deer is the main prey of the mountain lion, as it eats about one deer a week. The mountain lion eats the deer and then goes to rest while the food digests. The mother mountain lion teaches her babies to hunt by practicing on rodents and rabbits.

The mountain lion makes its home in foothills, canyons, or mesa country. They live in brushy areas and woodlands where they can go unseen. Because people are starting to build homes up in these areas, there are more and more contacts with the mountain lion.

What should you do if you see a mountain lion in the wild? Experts say that you should not run. They say that if you run, you will look weak and like an animal worth chasing. You should remain calm and slowly back away.

What does a mountain lion look like? The mountain lion is usually light tan or light cinnamon-colored with black-tipped ears. It also has a very long tail. The larger lions weigh about 150 pounds and can get as long as 8 feet. This is not an animal to approach in the wild.

## STORY QUESTIONS

1. A likely reason people are fascinated with the mountain lion is because . . .
   a. it is a fearless hunter.
   b. it can get as heavy as 150 pounds.
   c. it is called by a variety of names.
   d. it teaches its young to hunt rodents and rabbits.

2. Another word for *prey* is . . .
   a. prayer.
   b. characteristic.
   c. hunted.
   d. diet.

3. Why does the name "mountain lion" connote the feeling of fear?
   a. probably because the mountain lion lives near humans
   b. perhaps because the mountain lion is endangered
   c. probably because humans have been attacked by these amazing hunters
   d. because humans hunt the mountain lion

4. The mountain lion has different names, such as the . . .
   a. jaguar.
   b. puma.
   c. lynx.

# GECKO LIZARDS

Gecko lizards are part of the reptile family. The definition of a reptile is a cold-blooded animal that creeps by moving on the belly or by means of small and short legs. Did you know that a gecko lizard is the only lizard that has a voice? That's right. A gecko lizard makes a squeaking or clicking noise that sounds like "gecko." That's how the lizard got its name. Gecko lizards are nocturnal, which means that they are active during the night. This is why they have excellent vision.

Gecko lizards have sticky toe pads that allow them to climb well even on smooth surfaces. There is a type of gecko lizard that can fly through the air. These are called "flying geckos." These lizards have a flap of skin on the abdomen, which works like a bird's wing.

Gecko lizards can grow to be 14 inches long! The wide tail of the lizard helps store fat. The lizard has a long tongue that it uses to clean itself—especially the membrane that covers its eyes. These lizards are carnivores, which means that they eat meat. Crickets and cockroaches are a big part of its diet, but a gecko lizard will also eat young birds, eggs, and tiny mammals out at night. The snake is the main predator of the gecko lizard. If it is caught by the tail, the gecko lizard will let its tail go. The tail will flop and flail as the lizard gets away. The lizard will eventually grow another tail.

## STORY QUESTIONS

**1.** How did the gecko lizard get its name?

   a. its spotted back

   b. by the sound it makes

   c. where the gecko lizard lives

   d. the manner in which it eats

**2.** What is the meaning of the word *carnivore*?

   a. meat eater

   b. other lizards

   c. rodents and small mammals

   d. plant eater

**3.** How does the flap of skin help the flying lizard fly?

   a. It fights gravity.

   b. It emits a powerful force.

   c. It emits an odor in defense.

   d. It works similarly to a wing on a bird.

**4.** After reading the passage, which reptile below would you guess is most like the gecko lizard?

   a. snake

   b. horny toad

   c. tortoise

# THE JELLYFISH

Jellyfish are animals that live in water. Some jellyfish can live in fresh water, but most live in the ocean. The jellyfish is a mysterious animal. The jellyfish has a long body with long tentacles. These long tentacles are poisonous, and they sting. Some of the deadlier jellyfish have venom that can kill a human. The sunfish and the sea turtle eat the jellyfish and can do so without being harmed. The jellyfish eats mainly zooplankton and small shrimp in the ocean.

The jellyfish is made up of mostly water. In fact, 98% of the jellyfish is water. The smallest jellyfish are just a few inches long, while the largest jellyfish can be up to three feet long. The jellyfish gets its name from the jelly-like feel of the body.

Their jelly-like bodies are clear or sometimes have a pale coloring of blue, orange, brown, white, or pink. Some jellyfish may also come in other colors of deep yellow, deep blue, bright purple, pale lilac, bright orange, and deep red. If disturbed at night, some jellyfish give off a bright light. This makes them look like they glow in the dark.

## STORY QUESTIONS

1. Why does the author say that jellyfish are mysterious animals?
   a. They eat zooplankton.
   b. They are related to the sea anemone.
   c. They have unique bodies and they have a harmful sting.
   d. They are made up of mostly water.

2. What is the main idea of the second paragraph?
   a. the diet of the jellyfish          c. the color of the jellyfish
   b. the enemies of the jellyfish       d. the makeup of the jellyfish

3. What is the meaning of the word *disturbed* in the third paragraph?
   a. settled                            c. bothered
   b. unconcerned                        d. mentally unsettled

4. Most jellyfish live in the ocean, but where are some jellyfish found?
   a. in fresh water
   b. in the Indian Ocean
   c. in the sea
   d. in Niagara Falls

Name _____ Date _____

# THE WOMBAT

The wombat has an unusual name, and it is an unusual animal. It lives mainly in Australia and Tasmania. It is a marsupial, which means that it is a pouched animal that carries its young inside the pouch. The wombat is a nocturnal animal, which means that it is most active at night.

It is the largest burrowing mammal. The wombat burrows into the ground with its large paws and sharp claws. The pouch faces backwards so that the flying dirt does not get in the pouch. The baby wombat lives in the pouch for up to six months.

This heavy little animal shuffles as it walks. It has very short, stocky legs. The wombat ranges in length from two to four feet. The wombat is an herbivore, which means that it eats plants, bark, leaves, and roots. The wombat has coarse gray or brown fur, a large head, small ears, and a large nose. The wombat also has a strong back, which it uses to push intruders out of its burrow.

## STORY QUESTIONS

1. What would be another title for this reading passage?
   a. "The Wombat's Diet"
   c. "The Life of a Wombat"
   b. "The Wombat's Habitat"
   d. "Indigenous Animals of Australia"

2. Which paragraph explains the eating habits of the wombat?
   a. first
   c. third
   b. second
   d. none of the above

3. Locate the statement below that is a fact.
   a. The wombat is an adorable animal.
   b. The wombat is a nocturnal animal.
   c. The wombat loves living in a zoo.
   d. The wombat's legs are very long.

4. In this passage, the word *burrowing* means . . .
   a. searching for food.
   b. using one's nose.
   c. digging into the ground.
   d. rooting for bark, plants, and leaves.

# WALT DISNEY

Where is "the happiest place on earth"? Some say it is Disneyland! Do you know the person who created this amazing theme park? He was a man named Walt Disney. Walt Disney was a pioneer in motion pictures. He also created Mickey Mouse and the Disney World theme parks. Walt Disney received hundreds of awards from all over the world.

Walt Disney was born in Chicago, Illinois. He was raised on a farm in Missouri with four other siblings. Walt's parents, Flora and Elias Disney, encouraged his creativity and sketches and drawings. Walt sold his first sketches at the age of seven.

After serving some time in the Red Cross, Walt got a job as an advertising cartoonist. This was where he marketed and created his first animated cartoon. In 1935, Walt married Lillian Bounds. They had two daughters. Another important member of the family was brought to life in 1928. That was Mickey Mouse.

Walt perfected the combination of animation and sound. *Snow White and the Seven Dwarfs* was created in 1937. Since then, the Disney name has gone on to produce hundreds of animated movies.

## STORY QUESTIONS

1. What are the author's feelings about Walt Disney?
   a. indifferent
   b. disapproves
   c. unsure
   d. admires

2. Which sentence shows how the author feels about Walt Disney?
   a. Walt married Lilian Bounds.
   b. Disney was born in Chicago.
   c. Walt Disney perfected the combination of animation and sound.
   d. Walt got a job as an advertising cartoonist.

3. Which sentence is <u>not</u> an example of the encouragement Disney received through the years?
   a. He got a job at an advertising agency.
   b. He invented Mickey Mouse.
   c. His parents encouraged his creativity.
   d. He received awards from all over the world.

4. What is the meaning of word *pioneer* in this passage?
   a. trailblazer of new ideas
   b. worker
   c. traveled across the plains
   d. nomads

# HELEN KELLER

Can you imagine what it would be like not to be able to speak or hear?  When Helen Keller was 19 months old, she became very ill.  Doctors expected her to die, but she survived.  Helen's mother soon noticed that Helen was not responding when the dinner bell rang or when she waved her hand in front of Helen's face.  It then became apparent that Helen's illness had left her blind and deaf.  She was born on June 27, 1880 in Alabama, where she lived with her family.  She was frustrated and confused.  She didn't know what was going on in her world.  Her parents knew that they needed help.  They hired a tutor for Helen.  Her name was Anne Sullivan.

Success didn't happen right away.  But one day at the water pump, a breakthrough happened.  Anne spelled the word *water* in Helen's hand.  Helen began to catch on.  Suddenly, her brain was on fire.  She reached down to touch the ground, and Anne spelled the word *earth* in her hand.  She continued pointing and learning.  She learned to spell 30 words on that day.

By the age of 10, Helen had learned to speak by feeling her teacher's mouth when she talked.  Some people couldn't understand Helen, but she kept trying.  She learned to read French, German, Greek, and Latin in Braille.  Braille is a way for people who can't see to read.  Raised dots are used to represent letters and words.  Soon Helen could read, write, and speak.

Helen Keller went on to give speeches all over the world.  Most of the money she earned was given to the American Foundation for the Blind.  She met 12 U.S. presidents, wrote a dozen books, and went to college.  Helen Keller lived to be 87.  She continues to inspire many people worldwide.

## STORY QUESTIONS

1. Why was Helen Keller so successful in life?
   a. People felt sorry for her and took pity on her.
   b. She eventually got her vision and hearing back.
   c. She learned to overcome obstacles and work hard.
   d. She was able to meet 12 U.S. presidents and speak worldwide.

2. What can you learn about Anne Sullivan from reading this passage?
   a. She traveled the world to give speeches.
   b. She was diligent in her efforts with Helen Keller.
   c. She was blind herself.
   d. She was placed in an orphanage.

3. According to the passage, which of the following statements is true?
   a. Helen Keller was unable to overcome great obstacles to do great things.
   b. Helen Keller didn't have to work hard to succeed.
   c. Helen's parents made the right choice in hiring Anne Sullivan.
   d. Blind people can be taught how to read Braille, but not deaf people.

**Name** _____     **Date** _____

# BABE RUTH

On February 16, 1895, a star was born. A baseball star, that is—George Herman Ruth, Jr. He would go on to be one of the greatest baseball players of all time. At the age of seven, George's father took him to St. Mary's School. It was a reform school and an orphanage. George seldom saw his family after that. He was in trouble a lot at school. Brother Matthias took George under his wing and became a great supporter of young George.

George showed a natural talent for baseball early on. He was a great catcher and pitcher. Jack Dunn gave George his first baseball contract, which was to play with the Baltimore Orioles. The players called him "Jack's newest babe," and the name stuck. From then on he was known as *Babe Ruth*.

Babe Ruth stayed with the Orioles for only five months. At the age of 19, he was playing in the major leagues for the Boston Red Sox. Babe set many records. One of them still stands: He still holds the record for pitching 13 innings without a score. This game went on to be the longest complete game of the World Series. Babe went on to play for the New York Yankees. He set even more records. In 1920, his first season with the Yankees, he set a record of hitting 54 home runs. His greatest homerun was probably when he pointed to the outfield wall in Wrigley Field and hit what is believed to be the longest home run hit there—right where he had pointed. Babe Ruth deserves to have his name remembered in baseball for many years to come.

## STORY QUESTIONS

1. What does the phrase "take him under his wing" mean?
   a. hook him up with a pair of wings
   b. show him some tricks of the trade
   c. nurture and be a mentor for Babe
   d. teach him techniques that will help on the baseball field

2. What is a word that could be used to describe Babe Ruth?
   a. studious
   b. talented
   c. rugged
   d. honest

3. George's childhood could be described as . . .
   a. loving and caring.
   b. supportive yet strict.
   c. typical and normal.
   d. unhappy and unsettled.

# HENRY FORD

Born the first child to William and Mary Ford in 1863, Henry grew up on a farm in Michigan. He went to school in a one-room schoolhouse and helped do chores on the farm. At a young age, he was very interested in how things worked.

He left home at the age of 16 to work with a machinist. He did odd jobs after that until he married Clara Bryant. At that point, he ran a sawmill. Finally, in 1891, he became an engineer at the Edison Illuminating Company in Detroit. He worked up through the ranks, which allowed him free time to work with engines. He created his own quadricycle, which was a bike on four wheels.

Ford went on to accomplish his dream of owning his own company and making his own car. In 1908, he introduced the Model T, but cars were still too expensive for most people. Ford invented the moving assembly line, which allowed him to make cars that were inexpensive, reliable, and efficient. Ford is credited with making the United States a nation of cars. His company is still around today. It is the Ford Motor Company.

## STORY QUESTIONS

*1.* What interests did Henry Ford have?

    a. learning how an airplane worked

    b. running a sawmill

    c. learning how things work

    d. building a car with good gas mileage

*2.* Ford probably became a machinist's apprentice so he could . . .

    a. be trained in how to work machines.     c. be taught how to build cars.

    b. teach how to work machinery.     d. learn about the history of automobiles.

*3.* What is the meaning of the word *credited* in the last paragraph?

    a. added to

    b. known for

    c. increasing debt

*4.* What is the main idea of paragraph three?

    a. Ford's invention of the quadricycle led to the car.

    b. Ford was trained by a machinist.

    c. Ford's cars were too expensive for people.

    d. Ford's ideas and creativity made cars popular.

**DAILY** Warm-Up 5   Name _____  Date _____

# LAURA INGALLS WILDER

The *Little House* books tell the story of Laura Ingalls Wilder and her family. Laura traveled with her parents and her sister, Mary, in a covered wagon across many states, including across the Indian Territory. They traveled around a lot. They set up a home each time they moved. Each place had different problems to face, but they worked together as a family.

Laura was born many years ago, in 1867. That was before there was electricity, cars, or television. Her family fought off grasshoppers, storms, dust, food shortages, and more. Laura's older sister, Mary, suffered a stroke and lost her eyesight. Laura's baby brother, Freddy, got sick and died. Another sister, Grace, was soon born into the family. It was a time of sacrifice for everyone. But the family stuck together. They learned to enjoy life, have fun, and make the best of it.

Laura went on to school and studied hard. She became the top student of the class and became a teacher. Laura went on to marry Almanzo Wilder. It was their daughter, Rose, who encouraged Laura to write her stories. These stories were published in a book that was instantly loved worldwide.

## STORY QUESTIONS

1. What type of stories are the *Little House* books?
   a. historical fiction
   b. mystery
   c. science fiction
   d. fantasy

2. What conclusions can be drawn about the Ingalls family?
   a. They were religious and dedicated to missionary work.
   b. They were wealthy and lived a life of luxury.
   c. They were hard working and persevering.
   d. They were lazy and undetermined.

3. Which statement best explains why Laura's books were so well received?
   a. They were filled with adventure and real-life experiences.
   b. People had the same experiences that Laura had.
   c. These books were written in first person.
   d. The content in the books is factual information.

4. What is the meaning of the phrase "stuck together" in the passage?
   a. They were connected and couldn't get apart.
   b. They were willing to sacrifice and get sick together.
   c. They didn't like their neighbors much, so they spent time together as a family.
   d. They didn't give up or turn away when times were tough.

# CLAUDE MONET

Claude Monet was a famous painter. You have probably seen some of his paintings. Monet was born in 1840 in Paris, France. His mother died in 1857. Life was not easy for him, but he had talent. His talent helped him throughout his life. His art began in drawing little cartoon pictures. A man by the name of Boudin noticed Monet's talent and gave him his first painting lesson. He was the one who encouraged Monet to paint outdoors. His family was not very happy about his job as a painter.

Monet had to go to Northern Africa, but when he got back, he went to Paris to get some more painting lessons. Monet's paintings are famous for their impression of light. Most of his paintings were painted outdoors. In this time, most painting was done inside in a studio. Painting outdoors was a new idea with painting. The type of painting that he was doing is called Impressionism. More and more people began to like this style of painting.

Monet had bad eyesight and other health problems. This made it difficult to paint. But he painted until the day he died. One of his most famous paintings is of water lilies. Monet died of lung cancer at the age of 83.

## STORY QUESTIONS

1. How did drawing outdoors change the way painting was done?
   a. The paint dried out more easily, and so it was expensive.
   b. Painting outdoors allowed painters to use natural light in their artwork.
   c. Painting was done using darker colors.

2. Why were paintings done outdoors unusual?
   a. They captured the light.
   b. They portrayed the countryside.
   c. Most paintings during this time were done indoors.
   d. You were paid more for paintings done outside.

3. After reading the passage, what can you infer about why Monet's parents were disappointed with his decision to paint?
   a. They wanted him to keep drawing cartoon pictures.
   b. They didn't think it was the right job for him.
   c. They didn't think it would be good for his health
   d. They didn't think highly of his teacher Boudin.

4. Which statement does <u>not</u> explain what made Monet such a good artist?
   a. Monet loved to paint outdoors and use light in his paintings.
   b. Monet was trained by Boudin and encouraged to paint outdoors.
   c. Monet had little support from his parents.
   d. Monet painted to the last day of his life.

# DR. SEUSS

On March 2, 1904, Theodore Seuss Gisel was born. Does that name sound familiar? Later in life he was known as Dr. Seuss, even though he was not a doctor. Many people felt that his books were like medicine. Dr. Seuss was a famous children's book author who wrote many books. These beloved books have been read by millions of children. You've probably read many of his books, as well.

Do you remember reading a story about green eggs and ham? How about a book about Horton who hatched an egg? These books capture the rhyming sounds of words and letters. Often, Dr. Seuss would make up words to go in his books. His books are also filled with creative and interesting creatures. Many of these creatures have been made up, but they seem real!

In the 1950s, there was a concern that children were not reading books because they found books boring. A publisher sent Dr. Seuss a list of important words for young readers. He wanted him to write a book that was fun and entertaining using these words. That was how *The Cat in the Hat* was born. Dr. Seuss went on to write many books that were both fun to read and entertaining. He was a creative author who made an impact on millions of readers.

## STORY QUESTIONS

1. Another title for this reading passage would be . . .
   a. "Green Eggs and Ham."
   b. "Literacy for the Young."
   c. "Dr. Seuss: The Amazing Author."
   d. "Dr. Seuss and His Patients."

2. Some similarities that are found in all of Dr. Seuss's books include . . .
   a. rhyming and rhythm.
   b. words using all letters of the alphabet.
   c. free verse poetry.
   d. nonfiction facts and details about animals.

3. In the last paragraph, what does the word *impact* mean?
   a. targeted
   b. hit
   c. insight
   d. influence

4. Based on the information in the passage, how did Dr. Seuss get his name?
   a. Many felt his books were like medicine.
   b. He was creative and young.
   c. He went to medical school for a few years.
   d. He had a Ph.D. and was called Dr. Seuss.

# JOHN GLENN

John Glenn was born in 1921 and grew up in Cambridge, Ohio. He married his childhood sweetheart, Anna Castor. They had two children, David and Carolyn. He went to college in Ohio and then entered the Marine Corps. He flew planes in World War II. He also flew for the Air Force after the war and received several medals for his service.

In 1959, John Glenn joined NASA (National Aeronautics and Space Administration). NASA is where astronauts are trained to go up into space. He was one of the first Mercury astronauts. He piloted the first manned spacecraft that orbited Earth. After completing three trips around Earth, he became a national hero.

John also ran for senate in his home state of Ohio and won. He had tried to win a seat in office a few times before. He finally became a senator in 1974. He also won re-election in 1980 and again in 1986.

But John's time in space was not done yet. After many years away, in 1998 he went on a second space mission. He was 77 years old. He wanted to help do experiments. These experiments could help scientists learn what happens to older people in space.

## STORY QUESTIONS

1. Why do you think John was able to go into space again at age 77?
   a. He was going to die anyway.
   b. He had already had experience being in space.
   c. He was in good health.
   d. He had won the race as senator.

2. What is the main idea of the third paragraph?
   a. It introduces the main idea of the passage.
   b. It discusses John Glenn's experience as an astronaut.
   c. It discusses John Glenn's experience as a politician.
   d. It explains the experiments done in space.

3. A good way to answer question #2 above is to . . .
   a. reread the entire passage.
   b. reread the first paragraph.
   c. look for the words *astronaut* and *John Glenn*.
   d. reread the third paragraph and determine the main idea.

**Name** _____   **Date** _____

# ABIGAIL ADAMS

Have you ever heard of President Adams? You've probably heard of him twice. There were actually two presidents with the same last name. That's because they were father and son. The wife and mother of these two presidents was Abigail Adams. This was the first time anything like this happened. Abigail is one of the most admired first ladies.

Abigail was born in Weymouth, Massachusetts. She never went to school, but she was very smart. She raised four children. She also ran the farm, and was widely known for her fight for American independence. She was asked her opinion many times on events taking place during Colonial times.

Abigail's husband, John Adams, was elected president of the United States in 1796. He was the second president. He and his wife were the first to live in the White House. John was not reelected, and so he and his wife returned to the farm. Abigail lived a great life, but she would not live long enough to see her son, John Quincy Adams, elected the sixth president of the United States.

## STORY QUESTIONS

1. How does the author feel about Abigail Adams?
   a. She was a typical first lady.
   b. She was an intelligent and admired first lady.
   c. She died before she saw her son become president.
   d. She ran a farm and fought for American independence.

2. Which statement supports the author's opinion of Abigail Adams?
   a. She was asked her opinion on events taking place during Colonial times.
   b. Abigail Adams was the wife and mother of a president.
   c. She never went to school, but she was very smart.
   d. Abigail was the first wife of the president to live in the White House.

3. The third paragraph informs the reader about . . .
   a. Abigail's life on the farm.
   b. Abigail's life in Massachusetts.
   c. Abigail's work for American independence.
   d. Abigail's life as wife and later mother of the president of the United States.

4. Where might this information about Abigail most likely be found?
   a. in a book about the Revolutionary War
   b. in a pamphlet about the president of the United States
   c. on a website about the presidents of the United States and their wives
   d. on a website about bad women of the United States

**DAILY** Warm-Up 10  Name _____  Date _____

# ELVIS PRESLEY

Do you like rock and roll music?  A man named Elvis Presley helped create this type of music.  This music also made Elvis a star.  Elvis was born in Mississippi, but he was raised in Memphis, Tennessee. He liked to sing growing up but never really did much with it.  When he graduated from high school, he got a job driving a truck.

One day in 1953, Elvis went to the Sun Record Company.  He wanted to record a song for his mother. The president of the company heard Elvis sing, and he was impressed.  He offered a recording contract to Elvis.  Fans across the country loved his singing as well.  His songs were heard all over.

Another company named RCA signed a recording contract with Elvis.  This company released five of his songs at once.  He sold millions of records.  By 1959, he had sold 21 million records.  He was also in movies and went on tours to perform his songs.  He was the world's most famous entertainer of his time.

## STORY QUESTIONS

*1.* Where do you find out which company Elvis signed a deal with first?

    a.  first paragraph

    b.  second paragraph

    c.  third paragraph

*2.* The author probably wrote this passage to . . .

    a.  warn listeners of Elvis' background.

    b.  inform the reader about Elvis' weaknesses.

    c.  inform the reader of Elvis' history.

    d.  inform the reader of Elvis' love for singing.

*3.* How many records does the passage say Elvis had sold by 1959?

    a.  25 million

    b.  21 thousand

    c.  20 million

    d.  21 million

*4.* Which of the following statements is <u>not</u> a fact about Elvis Presley?

    a.  Elvis enjoyed singing.

    b.  Elvis grew up in Memphis, TN.

    c.  Elvis grew up singing and recording records.

    d.  Elvis was discovered when he tried to record a song for his mother.

# ELEANOR ROOSEVELT

A person who is often mentioned as someone who helped the poor and those in need is Eleanor Roosevelt. It has been said that Eleanor was as kind a woman as she was strong. Born in New York City, Eleanor was sent to England for school. When she came back to the United States, she started doing social work to help the poor. Throughout her life she always found ways to keep helping the poor.

Eleanor married her cousin Franklin D. Roosevelt in 1906. Together, they raised six children. Franklin came down with the illness polio in 1921. By this time, he was active in politics. He felt that because of his illness, he should step down. But Eleanor encouraged him to keep trying. He was elected governor of New York seven years later.

In 1932, Eleanor went across the country with Franklin as he ran for president of the United States. By the time he was elected, the country was in the middle of a depression. Once again, Eleanor worked hard to help the hungry and jobless people. During WWII, Eleanor helped the troops. Later, she was named a delegate to the United Nations. She spent the rest of her life aiding and helping those in need.

## STORY QUESTIONS

1. Where do you find out about Eleanor's work during World War II?
   a. end of the first paragraph
   b. in the second paragraph
   c. end of the third paragraph
   d. beginning of the third paragraph

2. The author probably wrote this passage to . . .
   a. inform the reader of President Roosevelt's time as president.
   b. inform the reader about Eleanor's time as first lady.
   c. portray Eleanor's support of Franklin D. Roosevelt.
   d. portray Eleanor's commitment to helping and serving others throughout her life.

3. What does the phrase "active in politics" mean?
   a. taking part in government
   b. finishing a term in politics
   c. president of a political party
   d. loves to discuss politics

4. Which of the following statements is not a fact about Eleanor Roosevelt?
   a. Eleanor was supportive of her husband's service to the country.
   b. Eleanor's background was similar to the disadvantaged people she helped.
   c. Eleanor was caring for the jobless and poor throughout her life.

Name _____ Date _____

# ALEXANDER GRAHAM BELL

Did you answer the phone today? You have Alexander Bell to thank for that. Bell was the son of a speech teacher. He had helped his father through the years and learned many things. He was taught how people learned to speak and hear. He used this knowledge to help deaf people learn to speak.

Bell was born in Scotland in 1847. The Bell family eventually moved to Canada. Bell moved on to Boston, where he continued his work with deaf people. He was trying to invent a machine that would help deaf people speak. His first success was when he sent a musical note over an electrical wire.

Bell kept working and experimenting. He invented a machine that was able to send and receive human speech. One day he spilled acid on his clothes. He decided to use his machine to send a "help" message to his friend. His friend got the message through the machine! The telephone had been invented. Some people thought that others had invented the telephone. The Supreme Court finally ruled in Bell's favor. Bell eventually got a patent for his invention.

## STORY QUESTIONS

1. Alexander Graham Bell would probably be most interested in which of the following inventions?
   a. microwave
   b. cell phone
   c. Braille
   d. car

2. According to the passage, how did Bell finally receive the patent for his invention?
   a. He waited the official 10 years for it to happen.
   b. He went to the patent office to get the official rights.
   c. The Supreme Court ruled in Bell's favor.
   d. He spilled acid on his clothes and called his friend for help.

3. What is the main idea of the passage?
   a. Through hard work and dedication, Bell was able to accomplish great things.
   b. how the telephone was invented
   c. how Bell's background proved helpful
   d. how Bell won the patent for the telephone

4. What was the original purpose of the machine Bell invented?
   a. He was trying to invent the microphone.
   b. He was trying to invent the telephone.
   c. He was trying to invent a machine that would help deaf people speak.

# JOHN F. KENNEDY

John F. Kennedy was the 35th president of the United States. He was a very young president. Many people liked his leadership style. John was born into a very wealthy family. He was one of nine children. He went to private schools as a child and went on to Harvard University. World War II broke out and John was enlisted in the Navy. While at war, John was a war hero. He saved the lives of many men when their ship was hit.

After the war, he ran for senator of Massachusetts. He won by a huge margin. He served two terms. In 1960, he ran for president of the country. He debated against Richard Nixon. These were the first debates on television. John was elected president by a narrow margin. He was the youngest person ever to be elected president. He and his wife, Jackie, had young children in the White House.

As president, John worked hard to solve tough problems. He created the Peace Corps, as well as other programs. But not everyone approved. Kennedy was shot and killed in Dallas, Texas in November 1963. Police arrested Lee Harvey Oswald for the assassination of President Kennedy.

## STORY QUESTIONS

*1.* Based on the passage, what were some of John's interests?
   a. playing polo
   b. fighting in the military
   c. helping and serving others
   d. opening up talks with the Cuban leadership

*2.* What can you conclude about John Kennedy?
   a. He was loved and adored by everyone.
   b. He was able to accomplish many things in a short time period.
   c. He was learning to speak another language.
   d. He was the best president of the United States.

*3.* Which of the following items would not be on President Kennedy's resume?
   a. fought in World War II
   b. elected president of the United States
   c. served as a senator for Massachusetts
   d. arrested Lee Harvey Oswald

*4.* What is the main idea of the third paragraph?
   a. Lee Harvey Oswald was not mentally stable.
   b. President Kennedy was loved by some and despised by others.
   c. President Kennedy was the youngest person ever to be elected president.

# CHARLES LINDBERGH

The first person to fly alone across the Atlantic Ocean was Charles Lindbergh. Lindbergh loved to fly. He started flying at the age of 20. The following year, he bought his own plane. In the beginning, Lindbergh was a stunt pilot. He was paid to do tricks with his plane.

Then, Lindbergh began working as an airmail pilot. He delivered mail by airplane. He would fly back and forth between St. Louis and Chicago. Lindbergh was gaining experience flying long distances.

In 1926, Lindbergh began thinking about flying his plane nonstop from New York to Paris. This had never been done before. There was a prize of $25,000 for the first person who could do it. Lindbergh got a group of businessmen from St. Louis to help him. The first thing he did was buy a new plane. He named it the "Spirit of St. Louis." He set a speed record flying from San Diego to New York.

On May 20, 1927, Lindbergh accomplished the goal of crossing the Atlantic Ocean. It took him 33 hours. He was an instant hero and was given the Congressional Medal of Honor.

## STORY QUESTIONS

1. Which statement best explains the success of Charles Lindbergh?

   a. Lindbergh grew up in a wealthy family.

   b. Lindbergh learned to fly planes at an early age.

   c. Lindbergh had the talent, support, and courage to fly across the ocean alone.

   d. Lindbergh was motivated to earn a lot of prize money.

2. Which paragraph mentions the medal that Lindbergh was awarded?

   a. first paragraph          c. third paragraph

   b. second paragraph      d. fourth paragraph

3. Which statement explains the reason behind the name "Spirit of St. Louis"?

   a. Lindbergh was given financial support from men in St. Louis.

   b. Lindbergh was originally from St. Louis.

   c. St. Louis was the name of his wife.

   d. St. Louis was the place where the contest was held.

4. What is the author's opinion of Charles Lindbergh?

   a. unbiased and disinterested

   b. impressed and appreciative

   c. apathetic and interested

# OPRAH WINFREY

People throughout the world know Oprah Winfrey's name. But this was not always the case. Oprah was born in 1954 to Vernita Lee and Vernon Winfrey. She was poor and had an unstable family. She went to live with her grandmother. By her grandmother, she was taught to read at a very young age. She also began reciting poems and other pieces in front of her church congregation. Oprah's grandmother called her "gifted." Oprah didn't know exactly what that meant, but she thought it must mean she was special.

At the age of 19, Oprah got a job as a reporter for a radio station in Nashville. During this time, Oprah won beauty pageants and entered college at Tennessee State University. In 1976, Oprah hosted a television show in Baltimore. It was a success. Oprah stayed with the show for eight years. She left to start her own show in Chicago. In 1986, Oprah began the show entitled, "The Oprah Winfrey Show." It has been a huge success and has been running for over 20 years.

But Oprah has not just been a television personality; she has been an advocate for those in need. She gives out millions of dollars and has set up a network to raise money for the less fortunate. She has also pushed the importance of literacy and set up a book club to encourage reading. She continues to have high ratings and huge success across the world.

## STORY QUESTIONS

1. What is the purpose of the passage?
   a. to inform the reader about the history of television
   b. to instruct the reader on how to be successful on television
   c. to paint a brief picture of the life of Oprah Winfrey
   d. to share Oprah Winfrey's interest in television

2. What is the meaning of the word *gifted* as used in the passage?
   a. talented and exceptional
   b. special and special needs
   c. bestowed with a gift to help others
   d. endowed with a lot of money

3. What is the main message in this passage about Oprah Winfrey?
   a. Know what you want to be early in life.
   b. Plan big for great things might happen.
   c. Don't give up even when things are hard.
   d. Work as hard as you can at an early age to earn a large amount of money.

4. Oprah Winfrey is known for . . .
   a. her hard work in wealthy areas.
   b. her interest in literacy and helping others.
   c. setting up the Peace Corps.

Name _____ Date _____

# JESSE OWENS

One of the best track and field athletes of all time was Jesse Owens. Jesse's talent and abilities still inspire many people. Jesse set his first record in junior high school. By high school, he was known across the nation. He decided to attend college in Ohio. While competing in college track-and-field meets, Jesse broke three world records and tied a fourth. He was on fire! It took 25 years before anyone broke the running broad-jump record he set at that time.

A year later, Jesse was able to compete in the Olympic Games held in Berlin. The year was 1936, and during that time Adof Hitler was building up the Nazi Party in Germany. That year, Hitler said that no black person could possibly beat his "Master Race" athletes. Hitler couldn't have been more wrong. Jesse set records at this Olympics while at the same time beating Hitler's athletes.

In that Olympics, Jesse tied the record in the 100-meter sprint. He ran on the 400-meter relay team and set a record. He also set new Olympic and world records for the 200-meter sprint and the running broad-jump. He was incredible! Hitler was very upset. He did not even stay in the stadium. He left so that he wouldn't have to see Jesse being awarded any of the gold medals he had won.

## STORY QUESTIONS

1. What is the author's purpose of writing about Jesse Owens?
   a. to share the facts about Jesse Owens
   b. to share the inspiring story of Jesse Owens
   c. to point out Hitler's rude behavior at the Olympics
   d. to list all the medals Jesse won

2. Which sentence from the passage shares how the author feels about Jesse Owens?
   a. Jesse tied the record in the 100-meter sprint.
   b. He also set new Olympic and world records for the 200-meter sprint and running broad jump.
   c. He was incredible!
   d. By high school, he was known across the nation.

3. Which of the following statements did <u>not</u> happen in Jesse's lifetime?
   a. Jesse learned to run fast at a very young age.
   b. Jesse was born with natural talent and skill.
   c. Jesse was finally accepted by Hitler as the winner.
   d. Jesse broke many Olympic and world records.

4. Which would be the best title for this passage?
   a. "Hitler vs. Owens"
   b. "The 1936 Olympics"
   c. "Greatest Runner of All Time"
   d. "The Inspiring Life of Jesse Owens"

# BOSTON TEA PARTY

In the year 1773, there was a lot of tension between the American colonies and Britain. Britain was trying to control the colonies, but the people of the colonies were trying to fight British control. The British passed a tea act, which they felt would force the people of the colonies to buy their tea. The British sold the tea at a very cheap price. This way, they could also tax them for the tea. The British sent ships with tea to America.

As three ships filled with tea came into Boston Harbor, the colonists demanded that the leader of the colony make the ships leave. But the leader of the colony refused to do this. The people who lived there decided to take care of the boats themselves. In the middle of the night, a group of men dressed as Indians went aboard the ships. They threw all 342 chests of tea overboard into the water. People gathered along the shore. They cheered the men on. This famous event became known as the Boston Tea Party.

The King of England was upset. He did not like what the people in Boston had done. He helped pass a law to punish the men who dumped the tea into the water. This law only made the feelings between the two groups more tense. The British kept trying to control the colonies, and the colonies kept refusing. This was one of the significant events that led up to the Revolutionary War.

## STORY QUESTIONS

1. Which statement best explains the reason for the Boston Tea Party?
   a. The colonists were celebrating their taxes.
   b. The colonists were starting a new tradition.
   c. The colonists were exercising and demonstrating their independence from England.
   d. The colonists were upset with the leader of the colony.

2. Where in the passage does it explain the response of the King of England?
   a. first paragraph
   b. end of the second paragraph
   c. second paragraph
   d. beginning of the third paragraph

3. Which statement explains the reason behind the name *Boston Tea Party*?
   a. The refreshment at the party was tea.
   b. The tea party took place in Boston.
   c. The name is a way to show defiance to England.
   d. All the colonists were delivered free tea from the King of England.

4. What is the author's opinion of the Boston Tea Party?
   a. unbiased and disinterested
   b. impressed and appreciative
   c. you can't tell from reading the passage
   d. supportive and encouraging

# SEGREGATION

In the 1950s, the South was very segregated. This meant that black and white people were not allowed to do anything together. They weren't encouraged to interact together in any setting. It was a sad and absurd time in the South.

Laws were in place that made blacks attend separate schools and separate churches. They were not allowed to eat at the same restaurants as white people. They were not allowed to sit next to the whites on the bus or the train. If there were not enough seats for whites, black people were required to give up their seats.

In public places, the whites and blacks had separate drinking fountains. African-Americans were not even allowed to vote. This had to stop. But changes came very slowly.

Many people helped bring about these changes. Jackie Robinson showed the world that black people had great talent. Thurgood Marshall fought for equal education rights for children. Rosa Parks refused to give up her seat on a bus. Dr. Martin Luther King, Jr. took the message to Washington, D.C. and gave his famous speech. These and many more people helped bring about the much-needed changes.

## STORY QUESTIONS

1. How does the author feel about segregation?
   a. disgusted
   b. amused
   c. understanding
   d. anxious

2. Which statement shows the author's opinion of segregation?
   a. Rosa Parks refused to give up her seat on a bus.
   b. Dr. Martin Luther King, Jr. took the message to Washington, D.C.
   c. It was a sad time in the South.
   d. But changes came very slowly.

3. The second and third paragraphs inform the reader about . . .
   a. the discrimination against people living in the South.
   b. the differences between the rich and the poor.
   c. the discrimination between the immigrants and the slaves.
   d. the discrimination against the blacks in the South.

4. Where would this information about segregation most likely be found?
   a. in a book about the Revolutionary War
   b. in a pamphlet about the president of the United States
   c. on a website about the Civil War
   d. on a website about civil rights

**DAILY** Warm-Up 3   Name _____   Date _____

# PEARL HARBOR

World War II was a time of great sorrow for countries around the world. Many countries in Europe were fighting against one another. The United States had managed to stay out of the war, but that soon changed.

On December 7, 1941, warplanes from Japan made a surprise attack on a naval base near Pearl Harbor, Hawaii. The results were deadly. More than 2,400 Americans were killed. Many warships were destroyed. It was a terrible day for the United States.

Japan attacked the United States because it had stopped selling needed goods to Japan. Japan was angry about this and decided to attack the United States.

The day after the attack, the United States declared war on Japan. Three days later, Germany and Italy declared war on the United States because they were friends with Japan. The United States became part of the war alongside Britain and the Soviet Union. Many more people were killed in World War II. It was one of the deadliest wars of all time.

## STORY QUESTIONS

1. A different title for this reading passage could be . . .
   a. "Beginnings of World War II."
   b. "Adolf Hitler's Power."
   c. "Pearl Harbor Attacked."
   d. "V-Day and Pearl Harbor."

2. A similarity between the attacks on Pearl Harbor and the terrorist attacks in New York City on September 11, 2001 is . . .
   a. the fact that they were both surprise attacks.
   b. that they were both attacks from Asian countries.
   c. that they both took place in December.
   d. that they took place when the United States was at war.

3. In the last paragraph, what does the word *deadliest* mean?
   a. most people targeted
   b. most people killed
   c. most people shot
   d. most people involved

4. Based on the information in the passage, why was Pearl Harbor attacked?
   a. Japan was trying to get the U.S. involved in World War II.
   b. The U.S. had bombed Japan.
   c. Adolf Hitler asked Japan to do it.
   d. Japan was upset with some decisions the U.S. made about selling goods to their country.

# MAN ON THE MOON

The space race was on to see which country would be the first to put a man on the moon. The U.S.S.R. had put the first satellite into space. It was called *Sputnik*. The United States was working hard to get a man on the moon. It was a tough goal. This had never been done before. After years and years of hard work, it finally happened.

Neil Armstrong was the first man ever to step on the moon. His famous words were, "That's one small step for man, one giant leap for mankind." The date was July 20, 1969. Pictures and stories of this famous and historic event were found in newspapers around the world. There were pictures of the astronauts' footprints on the moon. Millions of people watched the event on television.

Buzz Aldrin was also with Armstrong on the voyage to the moon. Each of them spent hours on the moon doing tests and taking samples. The surface of the moon was fine and powdery. There is little gravity on the moon, so the two men were able to walk and hop freely on the surface. They also posted the American flag on the moon. There is no wind on the moon, so their footprints might still be there!

## STORY QUESTIONS

1. What type of accomplishment was putting a man on the moon?
   a. general accomplishment
   b. sad accomplishment
   c. difficult accomplishment
   d. disappointing accomplishment

2. What conclusions can be drawn about the first trip to the moon?
   a. It was a mission fraught with arguments and disagreements.
   b. It was a successful mission.
   c. It was an experience never to be repeated.
   d. It was an unorganized mission.

3. Which of the following statements about the moon is not supported by information in the passage?
   a. There is little gravity on the moon.
   b. There is plenty of water on the moon.
   c. The surface of the moon is fine and powdery.
   d. Neil Armstrong was the first man on the moon.

4. What is the meaning of the phrase "one giant leap for mankind" as used in the passage?
   a. It was a huge accomplishment and learning opportunity for humankind.
   b. It was an example of their willingness to sacrifice for humankind.
   c. Humankind would soon be making those same steps.
   d. There was not a lot learned from the experience.

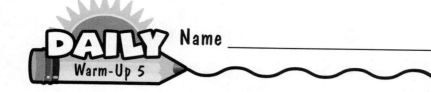

**Name** _____ **Date** _____

# THE GETTYSBURG ADDRESS

Perhaps the most famous battle of the Civil War was the one in Gettysburg, Pennsylvania. At the end of the battle, over 50,000 soldiers were wounded, missing, or killed. The Union and Confederate armies had each lost thousands of men. Many of the bodies were buried in shallow graves along the battlefield. The Union army wanted to do better than that.

The Union army was able to get land for a cemetery in Gettysburg. This cemetery was dedicated in November of that year. Edward Everett was asked to speak at the dedication. He was a great speaker of that time. President Abraham Lincoln was also asked to speak. He was the president during the Civil War.

On the day of the dedication, Mr. Everett spoke for two hours. When it was President Lincoln's turn, he spoke for two minutes. He didn't think it was a very good speech, but it went on to be considered one of the greatest speeches of all time. It became known as the Gettysburg Address. In his speech, Lincoln talked about the "new birth of freedom." His words inspired many people then, and they continue to inspire many people today.

## STORY QUESTIONS

1. What would be the best title for this reading passage?
   a. "Mr. Everett's Speech"
   c. "Lincoln's Famous Address"
   b. "The Dedication of the Cemetery"
   d. "Union and Confederate Soldiers"

2. What conclusions can be drawn about the battle of Gettysburg?
   a. It was one of the deadliest battles of the Civil War.
   b. It was a pivotal battle at the beginning of the war.
   c. President Lincoln approved of the battle.
   d. It was fought in a poor location.

3. Which statement explains why President Lincoln's speech was so well received?
   a. It inspired people to keep fighting.
   b. It inspired people to go home and think.
   c. It was used to encourage the wounded and dying soldiers.
   d. It inspired people to think about their freedoms and reasons for fighting.

4. What is the meaning of the phrase "new birth of freedom" in the passage?
   a. It is the idea that we are connected and shouldn't pull apart.
   b. It is a willingness to sacrifice and stick together.
   c. It is the idea that there was a new idea of freedom coming to light.
   d. It is the idea that you should never give up or turn away when times are tough.

Name _____   Date _____

# THE STAR-SPANGLED BANNER

Did you know that "The Star-Spangled Banner" is our national anthem?  This song has inspired millions of Americans and continues to inspire them today.  But how did this song come about?  The song was written by Francis Scott Key.  A battle between the colonists and the British was raging at Fort McHenry.  Key quickly wrote out a poem.  He was inspired by the flag flying over Ft. McHenry.  His poem had five verses.  We only sing the first verse in the national anthem.

"The Star-Spangled Banner" did not become the national anthem right away.  There was no music to the words.  Key scribbled the words to the poem on the back of a letter.  He also gave it its title.  He brought it back to Baltimore, and it was later published in the newspaper.  The words were then bought and published to the tune of the song "To Anacreon in Heaven."

This song did not gain in popularity for many years.  "Yankee Doodle" and other songs were sung more frequently.  "The Star-Spangled Banner" became more popular before the Civil War.  It was made the national anthem in 1931.  Today when this song is sung, people rise to their feet and put their right hands over their hearts.  This is to show respect for the country and for the flag.

## STORY QUESTIONS

*1.* What could be another title for this reading passage?
   a. "The National Past Time"
   b. "The National Anthem"
   c. "The Life of Francis Scott Key"
   d. "Respect for the National Anthem"

*2.* Which paragraph explains where the song was first published?
   a. first                         c. third
   b. second                        d. none of the above

*3.* Which statement below is <u>not</u> a fact?
   a. The national anthem is still sung today.
   b. Francis Scott Key wrote the song first as a poem.
   c. Francis Scott Key wrote the song "To Anacreon in Heaven."
   d. The national anthem was made official in 1931.

*4.* In this passage, the word *anthem* means . . .
   a. to show respect.
   b. original song.
   c. song created from a poem.
   d. song of praise.

**Name** _____ **Date** _____

# THE NEW ENGLAND COLONIES

The people of the New England colonies were Puritans. Like the Pilgrims, the Puritans in England were unhappy with the Church of England. They felt that they weren't able to practice their religion freely and live the life they desired. They wanted to travel to America to live this life. The Puritans formed their own stock company. More than a thousand men, women, and children left England to begin their new life in America.

The Puritans built their settlement in Boston, Massachusetts. Unlike many of the other newcomers, the Puritans were very successful. They didn't come with a plan to get rich from the gold they might find. They came prepared to plant crops and build homes. They arrived in America at a good time in the year so that their crops could grow strong. They had plenty of food to last throughout the winter. There were not very many Puritans who died as a result of the winter.

People back in England learned how successful the Puritans were, so more and more people came to set up colonies. For many of these people, life was a struggle in England. They wanted to come to America for a better life. The Puritans set up laws for the colony. They were very religious people. Not all of the newcomers agreed with the Puritan way of life. Some of these people were forced to leave, and they set up new settlements. More and more people continued to travel to America. The colonies continued to grow.

## STORY QUESTIONS

1.  What was the purpose of the Puritans settling the New England colonies?
    a. to stabilize the immigrants traveling to the United States
    b. to obey the law established by the King of England
    c. to practice their religion freely
    d. to aid other Puritans

2.  Identify a supporting detail that explains the statement, "They were very religious people."
    a. The Puritans worshipped in the Church of England.
    b. The colonies continued to grow.
    c. More and more people continued to travel to America.
    d. Not everyone was pleased with the Puritan's way of life.

3.  After reading the passage, which question could you answer about the Puritans?
    a. Who were the Puritans, and what are they known for?
    b. How many different types of Puritan congregations are there?
    c. What are the beliefs of a Puritan?
    d. What is the Puritan religion like today?

# ELLIS ISLAND

For millions of immigrants, Ellis Island was a symbol of hope and freedom.  Between 1892 and 1954, a very large number of people came to the United States.  They came for a new life.  There were over 12 million immigrants during this time.  The largest wave of people came in the year 1907.

Ellis Island is located just off the New Jersey shore in the New York Harbor.  Ellis Island was set aside as the immigration center.  The name came from Samuel Ellis who owned the island in the 1770s.

In the beginning, Ellis Island was used as a place to fight the British.  As the colonists fought the British, it was used as a defense post before the British arrived in New York Harbor.  Later, Ellis Island was used as a staging place for the new immigrants.  The ships would come and deliver people there.  Doctors would check for illness and disease.

A ship's manifest listed all the names of the people on board.  Sometimes the workers could not read the foreign names, and so they wrote down a different last name for those people.  Many people had their names changed by clerks on the island.

For some people, Ellis Island was known as the "Island of Tears."  Not all people were allowed to enter the United States.  If they had a contagious disease or the person seemed to be a concern, they were forced to stay on the island and work.  Some were even sent home.  Most people made it through the island in just a few hours.

## STORY QUESTIONS

1. Another title for this reading passage could be . . .
   a. "Island Paradise."
   c. "Island of Tears."
   b. "Problems of Immigration."
   d. "The Immigration Island."

2. Why was Ellis Island also called the "Island of Tears"?
   a. People were injured at Ellis Island.
   b. Ellis Island was a cruel place.
   c. Not everyone was allowed to pass through Ellis Island to the United States.
   d. Immigrants were unhappy to leave their homelands.

3. The author wrote this passage to . . .
   a. justify keeping immigrations on Ellis Island.
   b. inform the reader of how immigrants were not mistreated.
   c. share general information about Ellis Island.
   d. raise awareness of mistreatment of immigrants at Ellis Island.

# ALASKA BECOMES A STATE

By the 1850s, most of the land between the Atlantic and Pacific Oceans was part of the United States. Much of the land to the north belonged to Canada. Land to the south belonged to Mexico. Land to the north was filled with plenty of fish and animals.

William Seward, who was Secretary of State, wanted the U.S. to buy some of this land to the north. Russia owned this land but was willing to sell it. The United States bought the Alaskan territory from Russia for $7.2 million.

Not everyone in the United States thought it was a good buy. Many thought it was too cold and that people wouldn't want to live there. The land was called "Seward's Icebox."

It wasn't until 1897, almost 50 years later, before Americans gained interest. That's because gold was found in Alaska. Thousands of people rushed to Alaska to find their treasure. Alaska also ended up providing the United States with minerals and oil. Alaska finally became the 49th state in 1959.

## STORY QUESTIONS

1. What interests did William Seward have in Alaska?
   a. He wanted America to expand and grow.
   b. He was offered a good land deal.
   c. It was filled with fish and animals.
   d. It would be a place for people to immigrate.

2. What of the following sentences is <u>not</u> a concern that people had about purchasing Alaska?
   a. Buying Alaska was a waste of money.
   b. People thought it was too cold.
   c. People wouldn't want to live there.
   d. Alaska was filled with oil.

3. What is the meaning of the phrase "Seward's Icebox" in the third paragraph?
   a. cold and freezing place bought by Seward
   b. place to store frozen foods
   c. place where ice is stored
   d. waste of money

4. What is the main idea of paragraph four?
   a. Many people thought Alaska was a bad purchase.
   b. The gold rush in Alaska boosted interest.
   c. Seward learns of his mistakes.
   d. Alaska is purchased by the U.S.

Name _____ Date _____

# WESTWARD, HO!

The size of the country was growing quickly. People were in search of land. Upon arriving in America, many headed west to settle. They were called pioneers. Pioneers were the first people to settle an area. The pioneers came across the mountains looking for good land.

Pioneers came by the thousands. Some traveled down the Ohio River, while others came down the Mississippi River. They traveled on flatboats. The flatboats could go through shallow places in the river without getting stuck. When enough people arrived, that state was given statehood. Kentucky and Indiana became states during this time.

As more and more people moved west, they encountered Indians. The Indians were not happy with the intruders. Tensions grew as the pioneers looked for new land and the Indians worked to keep their land.

## STORY QUESTIONS

1. People wanted to move west to take advantage of the . . .
   a. specific resources in the area.
   b. assignments they were given.
   c. land available to settle.
   d. opportunity to meet the Native Americans living there.

2. Another title for this reading passage could be . . .
   a. "Westward Returns Eastward."       c. "Confronting the Indians."
   b. "Problems of Immigration."         d. "Moving Westward."

3. What is the main idea of the passage?
   a. Pioneers traveled westward in search of good land.
   b. Indians were not happy with the pioneers.
   c. Pioneers were famous explorers.
   d. People moving west were looking for gold.

4. The flatboats were ideal because . . .
   a. they could carry a large load.
   b. they could maneuver through shallow parts of the river.
   c. they were more stable on the river.
   d. they were an inexpensive way to travel.

**DAILY** Name _____ Date _____
Warm-Up 11

# SOUTHERN PLANTATIONS

Most of the people who lived in the South owned farms. The South had a long growing season. This made it easier for farmers to grow food. This made it possible to have a cash crop, meaning they could sell their crops for money.

Soon, the farms grew into plantations. A plantation was about the size of 100 small farms. For some of the plantations, the cash crop was tobacco. Others grew rice or indigo.

To grow these crops, owners and farmers needed a lot of workers. Sometimes they had as many as 50 to 100 workers. Many of these workers at the time were indentured servants. They were working to pay off their passage to America. But soon these workers were replaced with slaves. Slaves were cheaper. Slaves were easier to control. Slavery rose to become a huge issue in the South for many years to come.

## STORY QUESTIONS

1. What is the author's opinion about the Southern plantations?
   a. tolerant
   b. pathetic
   c. disgusted
   d. You can't tell.

2. Which of the following sentences explains why indentured servants were replaced with slaves?
   a. Indentured servants were cheaper than slaves.
   b. Indentured servants were easier to control than slaves.
   c. Slaves were easy to locate.
   d. Slaves were cheaper.

3. Which of the following statements is the reason why cash crops were grown?
   a. Growing year round is easier.
   b. Plantation owners worked together to grow crops.
   c. Farmers could sell cash crops for money.
   d. The plantation owners wanted to eat certain foods year round.

4. What does the term "indentured servants" mean?
   a. slaves
   b. lazy people
   c. people who pay off money they owe by serving
   d. children who had jobs

**DAILY** Warm-Up 12

Name _____ Date _____

# WOMEN'S RIGHTS

For years and years, women had been fighting for many rights. Women were not treated equally to men. Laws were in place that did not allow women to vote.

After years of work, things were slowly changing. More and more women were finishing high school and going to college. By 1900, laws were being passed that allowed women to own property.

There were still needed changes. For example, jobs were divided into women's work and men's work. Women weren't allowed to have certain jobs, and they were still denied the right to vote.

Many women leaders worked to bring this right to all women. These women held marches demanding the right to vote. They wrote letters and made speeches to the nation's leaders.

Finally, in 1920, all adult women were given the right to vote. This was the 19th Amendment to the constitution.

## STORY QUESTIONS

1. Which paragraph explains when women were finally allowed to own property?
   a. first paragraph
   b. last paragraph
   c. third paragraph
   d. second paragraph

2. What inferences can you make about why women finally received the right to vote?
   a. They had been demanding it for years.
   b. They made convincing arguments in speeches and letters.
   c. It was only a matter of time before they would be given the right.
   d. Women had to demonstrate they were capable of voting.

3. What is the author's opinion about women voting?
   a. The author thinks that it was a great day when women got the right to vote.
   b. The author thinks there has not been enough research on women's voting rights.
   c. The author is interested in sharing the fascinating process of how to vote.
   d. The author is indebted to and feels happy that men allowed women the right to vote.

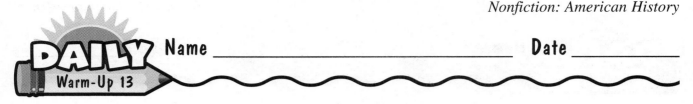

Name _____ Date _____

# THE DUST BOWL

The Dust Bowl is a term used to describe a region that suffered from drought and dust storms during the Great Depression. The Dust Bowl of the 1930s lasted for about a decade. It was one of the most trying times in the history of the nation. Families struggled to survive during this time. The Dust Bowl actually caused the Depression to last longer.

The Dust Bowl was located along the southern Plains. Oklahoma, Kansas, and parts of Texas, New Mexico, and Colorado made up the Dust Bowl. Drought took away the rains and the water. The land was left dry and parched. The wind came and blew the dust around.

The blowing dust made it difficult to do even simple things. It was hard to breathe, eat, and sleep with all the dust. People got sick from all the dust. Farmers were not able to grow crops. Food and water were scarce.

Sometimes the dust storms were so bad they were more like dust blizzards. One day was called "Black Sunday." On this day, the worst dust blizzard happened. It caused a lot of damage. The rains did not come until 1939.

## STORY QUESTIONS

1. How did the Dust Bowl get its name?
    a. The dust in the bowl kept spilling over.
    b. The land was filled with dust.
    c. The name was given when the country was struggling during the Depression.
    d. Dust and bowls were the two most common occurrences during that time.

2. What is the purpose of the third paragraph?
    a. to explain how the Dust Bowl was formed
    b. to explain how the Dust Bowl affected daily life
    c. to explain how Dust Bowls can be prevented
    d. to explain how people survived the Depression

3. Which paragraph would you read to find out about Black Sunday?
    a. first paragraph
    b. third paragraph
    c. second paragraph
    d. fourth paragraph

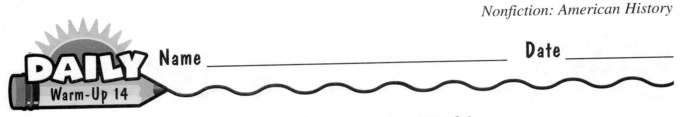

# LEISURE TIME IN AMERICA

In the early 1800s, Americans spent their whole day working. Sunday was the only day off, and the only vacation days were Christmas, New Year's Day, and the Fourth of July. People worked around 66 hours a week, which meant about 11 hours a day were spent at work.

By the 1950s, times had changed. People worked only 40 hours a week. The number of work hours per day was less, and most people had Saturdays and Sundays off each week. Most workers were also given two weeks of vacation time each year. People had a lot more free time.

Americans did lots of things with their free time. Many people watched movies. In the 1950s, the movies were now in color. People would drive their cars to a field with a big movie screen to watch a "drive-in" movie.

Many families also had their own television. TV was an amazing little box with pictures. Families sat down together at night to watch a TV show together. Shopping, sports, and traveling were other ways that people entertained themselves in their free time.

## STORY QUESTIONS

1. Which of the following statements is not found in the reading passage?
   a. The 1950s was a time of prosperity in the United States.
   b. People watched movies in their free time.
   c. Americans were working fewer hours during this time.
   d. People went to drive-in movies during their leisure time.

2. What inferences can you make about life in the 1950s after reading this passage?
   a. America was probably at war during this time.
   b. Tensions were high in the United States.
   c. The citizens were not happy with their president.
   d. Americans were enjoying a time of peace and prosperity.

3. Pick the answer choice that best completes the sentence, "Movies were now _____."
   a. fashionable
   b. inverted
   c. in color
   d. increasing in number

4. The purpose of the first paragraph is to . . .
   a. introduce the invention of color television.
   b. explain the differences between the life of a worker in the United States at this time in history.
   c. compare the amount of vacation days to present day.

Name _____ Date _____

# I HAVE A DREAM

Dr. Martin Luther King, Jr. was a Baptist minister. He lived in the 1950s and noticed that equality among people did not exist. People of color were discriminated against and treated very poorly. During this time period, the Supreme Court ruled on the case *Brown v. Board of Education*. This case was about ending segregation in public schools.

King fought for civil rights for all people. He made many speeches and marched in protests. He was trying to get the government to allow freedom to all people. King was eventually arrested and thrown into jail.

When he got out, he organized a march in Washington, D.C. On the steps of the Lincoln Memorial, he delivered his most famous speech. This speech talked about his dream that one day all children could sit and work together regardless of the color of their skin. His speech also talked about all Americans deserving the same rights.

Thousands of people heard this speech. This speech helped lead to laws like the Civil Rights Act of 1964. Dr. Martin Luther King, Jr. was, and still is, an inspiration to many.

## STORY QUESTIONS

1. What motivated Dr. Martin Luther King, Jr.?
   a. the treatment of the slaves
   b. the lack of equal rights for all American citizens
   c. the lack of representation for all Americans
   d. the misunderstanding of the government

2. Which paragraph would help you answer the previous question?
   a. second paragraph
   b. first paragraph
   c. fourth paragraph
   d. third paragraph

3. Which of the following statements is <u>not</u> true about Dr. Martin Luther King, Jr.?
   a. He was an inspiration to many.
   b. He fought for civil rights.
   c. He was an excellent physician.
   d. He was arrested and put in jail.

# JUPITER

Jupiter is the biggest planet in our solar system. It is 1,000 times larger than the planet Earth. That is pretty big! Jupiter is bigger than all the other planets combined. Jupiter is described as a big ball of gas. That is because it is made up mostly of gases. Jupiter is mostly hydrogen with a little helium.

We see mostly the outer layer of clouds when we look at Jupiter. Gas planets do not have a solid surface. The inner core of Jupiter is rocky and solid. Jupiter is the fourth-brightest object in the sky. People have been seeing Jupiter in the night sky for many years.

Many years ago, people thought Jupiter was a "bright, wandering star." A man named Galileo developed the telescope. The telescope helped him see Jupiter's four large moons. This observation helped Galileo realize that Earth was not the center of the universe.

The great red spot on Jupiter has been seen for over 300 years. This spot is big enough to hold two Earths. Jupiter also has rings. They are made up of particles of rocky materials. The rings are dark in color. Jupiter is the fifth planet from the sun.

## STORY QUESTIONS

1. What would be the best title for this passage?
   a. "Jupiter: The Largest Planet"
   b. "Outer Planets"
   c. "Cool Planets"
   d. "Planets with Moons"

2. Which of the following is <u>not</u> a fact about the planet Jupiter?
   a. Jupiter is the largest planet.
   b. Jupiter is one of the outer planets.
   c. Jupiter has a great red spot.
   d. Jupiter does not have rings like Saturn.

3. What was meant by the "bright, wandering star?"
   a. Jupiter was at first a star that moved across the sky at night.
   b. Jupiter couldn't be found in the night sky.
   c. Jupiter was located in a star's position.
   d. Jupiter was first thought to be a star that moved in the night sky.

4. How did the telescope change what people thought about Jupiter?
   a. Jupiter was the first planet viewed through a telescope.
   b. Galileo discovered that Jupiter had moons.
   c. It was determined that Jupiter was not located in a star's position.
   d. Jupiter was discovered to be the center of the universe.

# THE CENTRAL NERVOUS SYSTEM

The adult brain weighs about three pounds. This doesn't seem like much, but it is one of the most important organs in the human body. The brain is made up of millions of nerve cells. These nerve cells tell the rest of the body what to do. Without a brain, we could not live. The spinal chord is connected to the brain. It runs from our neck down through our back. The spinal chord and the brain make up what is called the central nervous system.

The brain is like the body's computer. It controls body temperature and reminds us to breathe. The brain allows the body to have voluntary movement, thought, language, and reasoning. Different parts of the brain have different jobs. The brain tells us when we are hungry and thirsty. It also is responsible for memory and emotion.

Our brain relies on food to give it energy. You need to eat healthy foods to keep your brain and the rest of your body working right. Healthy foods like fruits, vegetables, cereals, grains, milk, and other dairy products are all important foods for us to eat. We also need to keep our brains active. Research has shown that the less active our brain is, the less we are able to remember and do. So keep thinking, moving, and doing. It's great for your brain.

## STORY QUESTIONS

1. After reading the passage, what do you think would happen if your brain was injured?
   a. It would immediately double in size.
   b. Our bodies might not be able to perform certain things.
   c. The heart would begin to take over the body.
   d. Doctors have not yet determined what happens in this case.

2. The main idea of this passage is . . .
   a. to inform the reader about what happens when they are thinking.
   b. to inform the reader about the connection between the heart and brain.
   c. to inform the reader about how important healthy food is to the brain.
   d. to share general information about the brain and the spinal chord and how they work.

3. Where can you find information about the spinal chord?
   a. second paragraph
   b. not in the passage
   c. third paragraph
   d. first paragraph

Name _____  Date _____

# MERCURY

Did you know that Mercury is the closest planet to the sun? It is also the eighth-largest planet. This means that it is not a very big planet. Mercury has been visited by one spacecraft. The name of the spacecraft was the *Mariner 10*. It flew by Mercury three times. In many ways, Mercury is very similar to the moon. There are a lot of craters on Mercury. Mercury does not have any known moons.

When looking up at the sky, it is sometimes possible to see Mercury with a pair of binoculars around sunrise or sunset. The temperature on Mercury can be very extreme. It is so close to the sun that it gets very hot during the day, but very cold at night. Mercury is about 36 million miles away from the sun. As far as we know, Mercury does not have any water, and it is black and brown in color. Mercury rotates on its axis very slowly but orbits the sun very quickly.

The surface of Mercury seems to show that there may have been volcanoes at one time on Mercury. Mercury orbits so close to the sun that sometimes it can be hard to see. Mercury is never far from the sun in the sky. The glare of the sun is so bright that you can see Mercury best at twilight.

## STORY QUESTIONS

1. Which of the following statements is not found in the reading passage?
   a. Mercury is the closest planet to the sun.
   b. Mercury orbits close to the sun, so it is hard to see at times.
   c. Mercury is one-third the size of Earth.
   d. It is believed that there were once volcanoes on Mercury.

2. What inferences can you make about Mercury, being it is the closest planet to the sun?
   a. There are probably glaciers there.
   b. It is very hot in temperature.
   c. It is the most likely planet to have life on it.
   d. It is made up of all gases.

3. Mercury revolves very _____ around the sun.
   a. quickly                          c. steadily
   b. inverted                         d. slowly

4. The purpose of the third paragraph is to . . .
   a. inform the reader about Mercury's surface.
   b. inform the reader about Mercury's temperatures.
   c. inform the reader on how best to see Mercury in the sky.

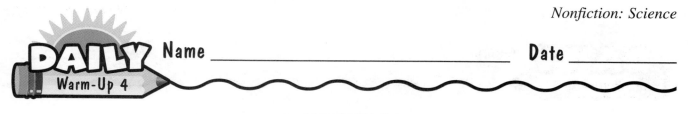

# URANUS

Uranus sits at the far end of the solar system, between Saturn and Neptune. These outer planets are made of very different material than the inner planets. Uranus is mostly made up of frozen gas. The inside of Uranus is made up of methane gas. The methane gas gives the planet a blue-green color. Uranus is also covered with clouds.

Uranus is the fourth-largest object in the solar system. It is the seventh planet from the sun. It has been discovered that Uranus has 27 moons and lots of rings. These rings are shaped differently than the rings of Saturn or Jupiter. Uranus has partial rings. The rings are very faint and hard to see. The moons are icy and have no atmosphere. There is not much possibility that there is life on Uranus.

The *Voyager II* flew by Uranus and was able to get 7,000 pictures of Uranus, its rings, and its moons. The *Voyager II* was launched in 1977 and arrived in 1986. That is one long trip!

## STORY QUESTIONS

1. What does the word *partial* mean?
   a. related to particles
   b. incomplete
   c. orbits the sun in one year
   d. see-through

2. Why did it take so long to get pictures of Uranus?
   a. Uranus does not have an atmosphere
   b. Uranus has just recently been discovered.
   c. It takes a very long time to get to Uranus.
   d. The *Voyager II* had difficulty getting to Uranus.

3. What does the passage say about how the rings of Uranus compare to the rings of Jupiter and Saturn?
   a. They are shaped differently.
   b. They are made up of different materials.
   c. They are longer rings.
   d. They are made up of methane gas.

4. Which of the following statements is not a fact about Uranus?
   a. It is the fourth-largest planet in the solar system.
   b. It is made up of methane gas.
   c. It has 27 moons.
   d. There is the good possibility of life on Uranus.

# EARTH'S ATMOSPHERE

What do you know about Earth's atmosphere? Earth's atmosphere is a thin layer of gases that cover the outer edge of Earth. It is mostly made up of nitrogen and oxygen. There are other gases in the atmosphere as well. This layer of gases is very important. It protects Earth from extreme temperatures. The atmosphere also traps heated air. It protects Earth from the sun's ultraviolet rays. These rays can be very harmful.

The atmosphere is about 300 miles thick. It slowly becomes thinner the farther it is from Earth and fades off into space. There isn't a real defined boundary between the atmosphere and space.

Oxygen in the atmosphere is important. Oxygen allows us to breathe. Without oxygen in the air, we would not be able to live. Some of the oxygen has changed over time. This is called the ozone layer. Some experts believe that humans have caused a hole in ozone layer.

The atmosphere is divided into five layers. The weather we experience on Earth takes place in the first layer. Weather happens because the atmosphere is constantly moving and changing.

## STORY QUESTIONS

1. Where does the weather we experience on Earth take place?
   a. in the atmosphere
   b. in the first layer of the atmosphere
   c. in the second layer of the atmosphere
   d. in the ozone layer

2. Which paragraph helps you answer the previous question?
   a. second paragraph
   b. first paragraph
   c. fourth paragraph
   d. third paragraph

3. Without the atmosphere, what would happen to Earth?
   a. It could not withstand the sun's ultraviolet rays.
   b. There would be no weather patterns.
   c. There would be less pollution.
   d. The ozone layer would not have a hole in it.

# EARTHQUAKES

Have you ever been in an earthquake? How did it feel? An earthquake can be a scary experience. What is an earthquake? An earthquake is really Earth's way of getting rid of stress. The earth has plates that shift back and forth. This stress and strain causes the surface of the earth to crack. It is like pushing against the two ends of a stick. The stick will eventually bend and break from the pressure. The earth's crust reacts the same way. As the plates move, they put pressure on each other. When the force is strong enough, the crust breaks. The stress is released as energy that moves through the earth in the form of waves. These waves are what we call earthquakes.

Did you know that there are different types of earthquakes? They are called tectonic, volcanic, and explosion earthquakes. A tectonic earthquake is the most common. These happen when the rocks on Earth's crust break because of the tectonic plates shifting. A volcanic earthquake takes place during the eruption of a volcano. Explosion earthquakes happen when there has been a chemical or nuclear detonation. These earthquakes take place in underground mines.

Earthquakes can be measured in many ways. One of the ways is to measure how intense an earthquake is. Magnitude is another way to measure an earthquake. The Richter scale is used to measure the magnitude. Seismic measurement is measured by using seismic waves.

## STORY QUESTIONS

1. Why are earthquakes likened to waves?
   a. Earthquakes begin out in the ocean.
   b. The waves of the ocean cause the earthquakes.
   c. The force of energy released when the crust breaks is called a wave.
   d. Nuclear chemicals form a wave.

2. What is the purpose of the third paragraph?
   a. to explain how earthquakes are measured
   b. to explain how earthquakes are formed
   c. to explain how earthquakes are prevented
   d. to explain how earthquakes are survived

3. Where would you read to find out about the three types of earthquakes?
   a. first paragraph
   b. end of the third paragraph
   c. second paragraph
   d. end of the second paragraph

Name _____ Date _____

# AMPHIBIANS

What is an amphibian? An amphibian is an animal that spends part of its life underwater and part on land. When amphibians are underwater, they breathe with gills. When they are on land, they breathe with lungs. They are cold-blooded. This means that their body temperature changes depending on the temperature around them.

There are three different kinds of amphibians. The first group is newts and salamanders. These animals are about three inches long. They have four legs and four "fingers" on each leg. They are red-orange and transform to the color green.

The second type is frogs and toads. Frogs and toads are very similar. Toads have a warty back and spend less time in the water. They eat insects and other small animals. Frogs begin as tadpoles. They spend time close to the water so that they can lay their eggs.

The last group is caecilians. These are worm-like creatures. Millions of years ago, there were other types of amphibians, but they are now extinct.

## STORY QUESTIONS

1. How is an amphibian different than most mammals?
    a. An amphibian eats different foods.
    b. An amphibian breathes underwater with gills.
    c. The amphibian is very territorial.
    d. An amphibian can swim.

2. Why is the word *fingers* in quotation marks in the passage?
    a. The author isn't sure it is the right word to use.
    b. The author is using it to show that they look and work like fingers.
    c. They don't become fingers until later.
    d. The author is unsure of what to call these things.

3. What are the similarities between a frog and a toad?
    a. They both eat insects and other small animals.
    b. They are both endangered species.
    c. They are both worm-like creatures.
    d. They both have tadpoles.

4. What does the passage say about some amphibians millions of years ago?
    a. There is not enough information about them.
    b. There are new species being discovered every day.
    c. They are now extinct.

# THE EAR

Did you hear that? If you did, then you heard it with your ear. The ear is a very important part of the body. Sounds can be soft or loud and the ear can hear almost all sounds. The ear takes in sounds, then sends this information to the brain. Ears also help you keep your balance so that you don't fall over.

The ear is made up of three main sections. These parts are the outer ear, the middle ear, and the inner ear. Each part of the ear plays an important role in hearing. The outer ear is the part that you can see. If you whisper in someone's ear, you are whispering into the outer ear. The outer ear holds the ear canal. This is where the wax is made. This earwax keeps infections from getting inside the ear. Earwax also collects dirt and keeps the ear clean.

Sound waves enter the ear and travel to the middle ear. Within the middle ear is the eardrum, which the sound waves strike and cause to vibrate.

The inner ear receives the vibrations into the cochlea. This is a small tube in the inner ear. The small tubes are filled with liquid. Tiny hairs line the tube. When the vibrations cause the hair to move, it creates nerve signals that the brain understands is sound. The brain understands the signal and hears the sound.

## STORY QUESTIONS

1. Which paragraph explains how the eardrum works?
   a. first paragraph
   b. last paragraph
   c. third paragraph
   d. fourth paragraph

2. What inferences can you make about the ear after reading this passage?
   a. Hearing is a fact of life for most people.
   b. Hearing aids are important tools for the elderly.
   c. Hearing is learned after the first year of life.
   d. The ear plays an important role in our being able to hear.

3. What is the author's opinion about the ear?
   a. The author thinks the ear can be used in a transplant.
   b. The author thinks there has not been enough research about the ear.
   c. The author is interested in sharing the fascinating process of hearing.
   d. The author is learning how the brain understands sound.

Name _____     Date _____

# INSECTS

Insects are animals that do not have backbones.  They have a hard exoskeleton, three body parts, two antennae, three pairs of jointed legs, and compound eyes.  Some insects have wings.  Insects hatch from eggs.  They also breathe through special holes called spiracles.

There are millions of different types of insects.  Insects are the largest group of animals.  Scientists say that insects have been around since long before the dinosaurs.  Insects are found all over the world.  They live on all continents, in backyards, and even in the walls of homes.  Insects live right alongside humans.

Many people are afraid of insects, but not all insects are harmful.  Insects may look scary to humans, but that does not mean they are harmful.  For example, daddy long-leg spiders, June bugs, dragonflies, moths, and butterflies are all harmless insects.

There are some insects that are harmful to humans.  These insects include centipedes, ticks, lice, bees, hornets, and mosquitoes.

## STORY QUESTIONS

1. Why do humans fear insects?
   a. They eat human food.
   b. They look scary.
   c. They are all dangerous to humans.
   d. They are more powerful than humans.

2. What is the purpose of the third paragraph?
   a. to explain how insects bite
   b. to explain how insects are hatched
   c. to explain how the insect body is constructed
   d. to explain that not all insects are harmful

3. Which paragraph would you read to find out about the types of harmful insects?
   a. first paragraph
   b. third paragraph
   c. fourth paragraph
   d. second paragraph

4. Which sentence explains how insects breathe?
   a. Insects breathe through their eyes.
   b. Insects breathe through special holes called spiracles.
   c. Insects breathe through the spiracles in their feet.
   d. Insects breathe through their antennae.

Name _____ Date _____

# THE CIRCULATORY SYSTEM

The circulatory system is an extremely important part of your body. This system transports blood throughout your body. At any given time, your body has five liters of blood flowing through it. The heart, the lungs, and the blood vessels all play an active role in blood flow.

Over the course of a person's life, the heart beats about 3 billion times. That is a lot of very important beats. The beating of the heart means that blood is being sent to the body. The heart is a muscle. It is a very strong muscle. It is divided into four main parts. The blood leaves the heart and enters the aorta. Fresh blood from the aorta goes to the brain.

The brain needs the oxygen in the blood. The brain could not live without this. Blood also travels through the lungs. Carbon dioxide is taken out and oxygen is put in its place. The arteries and veins take the blood to all parts of the body. The blood returns back to the heart through the veins.

You can hear your heart pumping blood in your body by using the stethoscope. One end of this tool is placed on your heart, and the earpieces go in your ears. The stethoscope works like a mini microphone so that you can hear the heart beating.

## STORY QUESTIONS

1. What could be a different title for this passage?
   a. "Blood in the Body"
   b. "The Heart and Lungs"
   c. "How the Circulatory System Works"
   d. "Arteries and Veins in the Body"

2. Which of the following is <u>not</u> a fact about the circulatory system?
   a. The heart beats about 3 billion times in the average lifetime.
   b. The blood contains oxygen for the brain.
   c. The blood returns to the heart through the veins.
   d. The brain helps the body move and have feelings.

3. What was meant by the use of the words "active role" in the first paragraph?
   a. Without the heart, the body would die.
   b. The brain, heart, and lungs are connected.
   c. The brain, heart, and lungs play an important role.
   d. The heart, lungs, and blood vessels work together to get blood flowing through the body.

4. How did the stethoscope help doctors learn more about the heart?
   a. They could hear the heart at work.
   b. They could use the stethoscope to measure the amount of blood flow.
   c. They could use the stethoscope to hear if a person has a heart or not.

Name _____ Date _____

# THE MUSCULAR SYSTEM

We all use our muscles to move our bodies. Without muscles, you would not be able to talk, eat, walk, sleep, or move at all. There are over 650 muscles that your body uses. These muscles are attached to the skeleton.

There are three types of muscles. They are the skeletal muscles, the cardiac muscles, and the smooth muscles. All of these muscles can tighten.

Some of these are voluntary muscles, and others are involuntary muscles. Voluntary muscles move only when we think about it. The muscles in our arms and legs work like this.

Involuntary muscles move when we aren't even thinking about it. The heart is an example of an involuntary muscle. If we had to think about it to make our heart beat, we might forget.

## STORY QUESTIONS

1. Doctors who work with the muscles would be most interested in a machine that . . .
   a. helps damaged muscles move.
   b. explains the function of each muscle.
   c. demonstrates how muscles work.
   d. takes pictures of muscles.

2. According to the passage, how do involuntary muscles differ from voluntary muscles?
   a. There is no difference.
   b. They work together to get the heart moving.
   c. We move involuntary muscles without thinking about it.
   d. Voluntary muscles move on their own.

3. What is the main idea of the passage?
   a. to show how muscles help us talk
   b. to explain the types of muscles and how they work
   c. to show how muscles help our body move
   d. to show how involuntary muscles work

4. What do the three types of muscles have in common?
   a. They are all involuntary muscles.
   b. They are all voluntary muscles.
   c. They carry the blood flow to all parts of the body.
   d. They are all able to tighten.

# TORNADOES

Have you ever been in a tornado? Have you heard about a tornado? Tornadoes are defined as a rotating column of air. A tornado can be weak, strong, or violent. Most tornadoes are weak. Only 30% become strong or violent tornadoes. A tornado usually comes down from a funnel-shaped cloud. The wind of a tornado can move as quickly as 110 to 200 mph.

Sometimes a tornado is called a twister. Some people like to chase tornadoes. They use equipment to measure how fast the tornado is moving. Unless you are an expert, you should never chase a tornado. You should not even get in a car during a tornado. The tornado can pick up a car and toss it aside.

What should you do to be safe in a tornado? A tornado can toss and throw things all over. It is important to get to a shelter. A tornado shelter might be in a basement or underground. The shelter needs to be sturdy and not a building that can be torn down by the intense winds of a tornado. Stay away from any windows or doors. Protect yourself from flying debris. All of these things can help you stay safe.

## STORY QUESTIONS

1. A likely reason people are fascinated with tornadoes is because . . .
   a. it is not known how they are made.
   b. they are a powerful force.
   c. it is a predictable weather pattern.
   d. it easy to follow a tornado.

2. Which of the following would be the best place to be during a tornado?
   a. in a strong building
   b. in a car
   c. in a tent
   d. under a desk

3. What is a reason to stay away from windows during a tornado?
   a. to avoid feeling the intense wind
   b. to avoid getting hit from flying debris
   c. to avoid being seen by the tornado
   d. to stay warm during the cold winds of the tornado

4. The tornado has different names such as . . .
   a. storm.
   b. disturbance.
   c. twister.

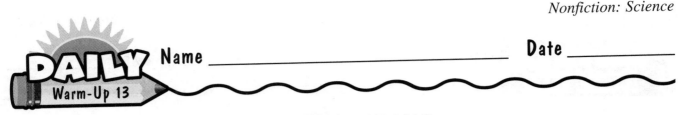

**Name** _____ **Date** _____

# CONSTELLATIONS

Have you ever looked up at the night sky and wondered about the stars? Did you know that these stars have been there since long before you were born? People have looked at the stars in the night sky for millions of years. Some of these stars seem to be in groups that form shapes. A group of stars is called a "constellation." Names were given to these groups of stars.

The best known group of stars is the Big Dipper. It is a group of seven stars. Three stars form the handle, and four stars form the dipper. The Big Dipper is actually part of a bigger group of stars called the Great Bear, or Ursa Major. Some say that this big group of stars forms the shape of a bear.

Another well-known group of stars is Orion. Orion was a Greek hunter from long ago. He wore a belt with different tools hanging from it. If you look closely, you can see Orion's Belt.

The Little Dipper is a group of stars that looks a bit like the Big Dipper. The North Star sits at the end of the Little Dipper's handle.

## STORY QUESTIONS

1. What is this passage mainly about?
   a. how the stars can be seen to form pictures in the sky
   b. how the stars were discovered in the night sky
   c. how each star was named
   d. how the Little Dipper can be found

2. Why was the constellation named the Ursa Major?
   a. It was not as small as Ursa Minor.
   b. It looked like a bear.
   c. It was one of the tools on Orion's belt.
   d. It is a constellation.

3. According to the passage, who was Orion?
   a. He was the leader.
   b. He was the king.
   c. He was a scientist studying constellations.
   d. He was a hunter.

4. Based on information in the passage, how can you find the North Star?
   a. Look for the Ursa Major.
   b. Look for Orion's Belt.
   c. Look for the Little Dipper's handle.
   d. Look for the constellations towards the north.

# VENUS

Venus is the second planet from the sun. Venus was named after the goddess of beauty and love. It is the sixth-largest planet. It has been known as the brightest planet. For millions of years, humans have noticed Venus.

The first spacecraft to Venus was in 1962. There have been many visits since then. The rotation of Venus is very unusual. It rotates very slowly and in a direction opposite that of the other planets. Venus is very similar to Earth. It is about the same size. They are also made of similar materials. The surface of Venus, however, has too much carbon dioxide to have any life.

Venus is quite dry. It used to have water (like Earth), but it has dried up. On the surface, Venus has slow winds. There are strong winds on the top of the clouds. Venus does not have a moon. Venus is almost always covered with clouds. The surface of Venus has small craters all over it. Venus also has lots of volcanoes on it. Venus is a fascinating planet.

## STORY QUESTIONS

**1.** What are the author's feelings about Venus?

  a. indifferent        c. unsure

  b. disapproves       d. interested

**2.** Which sentence shows how the author feels about Venus?

  a. Venus is a fascinating planet.

  b. Venus has lots of volcanoes on it.

  c. The first spacecraft went to Venus in 1962.

  d. Venus is the brightest planet.

**3.** Which question cannot be answered after reading this passage?

  a. How big is Venus compared to other planets?

  b. Is Venus similar to Earth?

  c. What is the temperature on Venus?

  d. How did Venus get its name?

**4.** What is the meaning of word *noticed* in this passage?

  a. wondered about

  b. been aware of

  c. recognized

  d. understood

# THE ASTEROID BELT

An asteroid is a piece of rock.  Most asteroids are made of rock, with some parts being nickel and iron.  Many people say that an asteroid is what was leftover after the planets were formed.  These rocks orbit around the sun.

Most of these asteroids are orbiting between Mars and Jupiter.  This is known as the asteroid belt.  It circulates as a belt of rocks around the sun.  Sometimes these rocks run into one another.  This changes their course and can break them into smaller pieces.

Some experts believe that these floating asteroids were actually part of another planet that never formed.  Some experts call them "minor planets."  It is said that if all of the asteroids were pulled together to form a planet, it would not be much bigger than the moon.  If one of these asteroids gets into the gravitational pull of a planet, it will orbit it like a moon would.

There have been times when an asteroid has fallen into Earth's gravitational field and crashed into Earth, but this is very rare.

## STORY QUESTIONS

*1.* Why does the author say that an asteroid hitting Earth is rare?
   a. It happens quite frequently.
   b. It can cause a lot of damage.
   c. It doesn't happen very often.
   d. It can be tracked using satellite photos.

*2.* What is the main idea of the second paragraph?
   a. what the asteroid belt is made up of
   b. the relationship between Mars and Jupiter
   c. what happens when an asteroid gets in the gravity of a planet
   d. the fact that an asteroid is a piece of a planet

*3.* What is the meaning of the term "minor planets" in the third paragraph?
   a. smaller or lesser          c. bothered
   b. unconcerned                d. unsettled

*4.* Most asteroids are made of . . .
   a. planets.
   b. stars.
   c. air.
   d. rock.

Name _____

Date _____

# THE OCEANS

What would it be like to live in the ocean? Many sea animals have found this to be the perfect place to live. Oceans cover more than 75% of Earth's surface. This means that the ocean is the largest habitat on Earth.

There are four oceans. They are the Pacific, Indian, Atlantic, and Arctic Oceans. The four oceans all connect to each other. There are also many seas. Seas are smaller branches of oceans. Some examples of seas are the Caribbean Sea and Mediterranean Sea.

Have you wondered why the ocean is salty? Rivers collect salt as they travel over rocks. The salt filters out into the seas and oceans. It dissolves in the ocean but doesn't evaporate. This means that the salt just builds up over time.

Waves on the surface of the ocean are caused by the wind. The stronger the wind, the stronger the waves will be. Waves only move up and down. Waves do not represent a flow of water.

## STORY QUESTIONS

*1.* Why is the ocean salty?

   a. Salt is generated in the ocean.

   b. The salt lies at the bottom of the ocean.

   c. The ocean collects salt from rivers.

   d. The waves create the salt.

*2.* What is the meaning of the word *dissolve*?

   a. build up

   b. encourage

   c. refuse to discuss

   d. dissipate

*3.* Why is the ocean Earth's largest habitat?

   a. It fights gravity.

   b. It emits a powerful force.

   c. It makes up 75% of Earth's surface.

   d. It is part of the Caribbean Sea.

*4.* Which of the following statements was not mentioned in the passage?

   a. The wind makes the waves.

   b. The waves only move up and down.

   c. The waves keep things in the ocean moving.

Name _____    **Date** _____

# CHILDHOOD OBESITY

These days, more and more children are overweight. A name for being extremely overweight is *obese*. Why is this happening? Doctors, teachers, and other adults believe that children are not getting the right amount of exercise and are not eating the right kinds of food.

In the past, children used to be more active. In early America, there was a lot of work to be done. Children helped on the farms and in the factories. Children didn't have much time to sit around. Today children go to school and come home to watch the television or play video games. Too many of their activities involve sitting and not being active enough. Children are not getting enough exercise, such as running, walking, or riding a bike.

Another main reason for children being overweight is the types of food they eat. More and more families are eating at restaurants or fixing quick foods that are loaded with calories. These types of food begin to add up day after day. Children are eating too many of the wrong foods and not enough of the right foods.

Some of the foods that children should be eating include fruits and vegetables, dairy, grains and cereals, and meat and poultry. These types of foods can help children maintain their weight and help the body fight disease.

## STORY QUESTIONS

*1.* Which of the following is <u>not</u> a reason why children don't eat enough healthy foods?

   a. Children eat more prepared foods than homemade foods.

   b. Children eat out at restaurants more than they used to.

   c. Children weigh more than they used to.

   d. Unhealthy foods are more readily available these days.

*2.* Which of the following statements would be the best one to be added to the passage?

   a. Children need to be taught about the foods they eat and the food choices they make.

   b. Parents are obese and overweight.

   c. Doctors are finding that more and more children are obese.

   d. Scientists are concerned about the food children eat.

*3.* What is the meaning of the word *maintain* in this passage?

   a. increase

   b. decrease

   c. think about

   d. keep steady

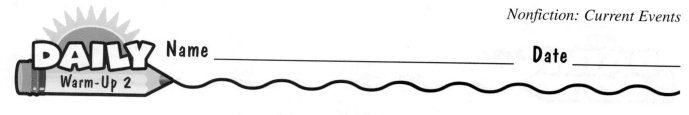

# LITTERING

It is very sad to see litter on the highways or in parks and other public places.  Littering is a big problem that needs to be stopped.  There is no reason why people need to litter.  Someone who litters is a lazy person.  It means he or she is too lazy to get up and throw away his or her own trash.

Many things have been tried to stop people from littering.  Laws have been passed to try to prevent littering.  If someone is caught littering on the highway, he or she can be fined to pay for it.  This seems to discourage some people, but certainly not everyone.

Littering can cause a lot of problems.  Littering can be harmful to the wild animals that live in the parks and forests.  Littering can kill animals or make them sick.  Sometimes food is left with trash and other things.  Wild animals eat this food, and then sometimes they get sick.  Littering also looks bad.  It's hard to enjoy nature when it is serving as a trash can for us!

## STORY QUESTIONS

1. What is the author's opinion about littering?
   a. tolerant
   b. pathetic
   c. disgusted
   d. annoyed

2. Which of the following sentences clarifies the how the author feels about littering?
   a. This seems to discourage some people from littering.
   b. It is very sad to see litter on the highways or in parks.
   c. There should be a fine for everyone who litters.
   d. Littering is more and more common today.

3. Which of the following is <u>not</u> an effect of littering?
   a. Littering is harmful to animals.
   b. Animals can get sick and die from litter.
   c. Littering looks bad.
   d. People can get paid if caught littering.

4. Who does the author blame for littering?
   a. the audience
   b. lazy people
   c. wild animals
   d. children

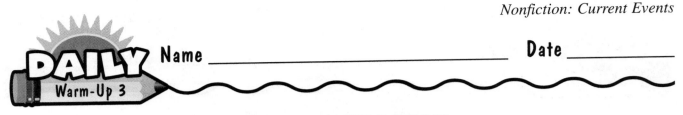

# TEACHER SELECTION

It would be a great idea to let children choose their own teachers. So many problems would be solved this way. Besides, children should have the right to choose the teacher that they think would best meet their needs. There should be a day set aside for students at the end of the year to meet all the available teachers for the following year. This could be a question-and-answer period where the students ask questions and the teachers answer. The teacher could also discuss his or her teaching style. Students could determine if they would be comfortable in that classroom.

Many students do not get along with their teachers. Other students are afraid of their teachers. Both of these issues get in the way of the student learning. If the student had more input on his or her teacher, school would be a happier place to be.

Of course the parents would need to be involved. The parents could also interview the teachers and ask questions. This would help alleviate many problems and concerns during the school year. There is the possibility that there would be students and parents who don't care who their teachers are. If this were the case, then these students would go wherever the principal felt like they should be placed. Teacher selection is an idea that needs to be considered!

## STORY QUESTIONS

1. Which would be the best title for this reading passage?
   a. "Choose Your Own Adventure"
   b. "My Education—My Choice"
   c. "Parental Requests"
   d. "Teachers Choose to Teach"

2. Which of the following is the main reason to choose your own teacher?
   a. Students would be able to select a teacher that meets their particular learning style.
   b. Parents would be more comfortable in school.
   c. You would get to choose the kids in your class.
   d. Students would be able to pick a teacher whom they have heard good things about.

3. What is meant by the phrase *teacher's style* in this passage?
   a. the way a teacher teaches and the classroom environment
   b. the clothes a teacher wears
   c. the way a teacher decorates the bulletin boards and classroom
   d. the way a teacher begins class each day

# CHARACTER EDUCATION

There has been a lot of talk lately about the importance of teaching values in the classroom. Values are characteristics such as honesty, kindness, hard work, and integrity. The classroom should not be responsible to make sure these ideas are taught. Schools should support these values, but they should not be held responsible to teach them. It is up to the parents to decide what values should be taught. This is the parent's job and right.

One reason is that the schools do not have time to teach all of the necessary values. Teachers barely have enough time to teach the subjects and topics they are already responsible for teaching. How would the schools decide which values to teach? There would be teachers who disagree with parents on what to teach.

Another reason is that there isn't enough money to take on this job. School budgets are already stretched too thin. Schools do not have the resources to teach values adequately. Students need consistent modeling and instruction on these life skills. Let the schools support these values but focus on the curriculum.

## STORY QUESTIONS

1. People who agree with this passage probably feel that . . .
   a. parents should take more responsibility in teaching their children.
   b. schools need more responsibilities.
   c. schools have enough money to teach values.
   d. teachers should receive more training and instruction.

2. The main question this passage asks is . . .
   a. When did values begin being taught in schools?
   b. Why doesn't the school teach values?
   c. Who should be responsible to teach values?
   d. If the school doesn't teach the values, how will students be taught?

3. _____ is an example of a value.
   a. Aggression                    c. Courage
   b. Passiveness                   d. Disagreement

4. Which of the following statements is <u>not</u> a reason why schools shouldn't be responsible for teaching values?
   a. Schools do not have enough teachers to teach values.
   b. Parents and teachers would disagree on which values should be taught.
   c. Schools are not aware of what values are.
   d. Schools do not have time or money to be responsible for teaching values.

# TOO MUCH TV!

How many hours a day do you watch television?  How many hours a week?  Most children watch way too much television.  If children are watching too much television, it means that they are not reading enough books.  They are probably not getting enough exercise either.  Watching television doesn't challenge our bodies mentally or physically.  It is a "brain dead" activity.

Television is also not good for children because many shows are too violent.  There aren't very many shows at night that could be considered children's shows.  Many shows that are made for adults are shown during the time when children are watching television.  It is not good for children to see so much violence.  Some researchers say that watching this kind of program on television leads some children to do violent things in real life.

Many children say that there is nothing to do but watch television.  This just isn't true.  Children can go on walks, take a bike ride, or learn how to cook.  They can play a game, do their homework, play jump rope, and do jumping jacks.  They can also play soccer, basketball, football, or dance.  There are so many things to do and so little time.  Children should turn off the television because they are missing out on too much fun!

## STORY QUESTIONS

1.  What is the main idea of the reading passage?
    a. Children enjoy free time outside.
    b. Children watch too much television.
    c. Television programs are too violent.
    d. There should be a way to block violent television shows.

2.  What is meant by the term "brain dead" in this passage?
    a. They are condemned.
    b. They are unsafe.
    c. They are not using their brains.
    d. They are torn down.

3.  According to the passage, why do children watch too much television?
    a. It is a requirement for families with small children.
    b. They are enticed to watch with the commercials.
    c. It is easier than reading or playing games.
    d. Television is a profitable industry.

4.  Which of the following statements is <u>not</u> a result of watching violent television?
    a. Children model what they see on television.
    b. Children are exposed to violence on a daily basis.
    c. Children are too young to watch some programs.
    d. Children learn from their parents how to treat others.

# SCHOOL UNIFORMS

Do you like to go school shopping each year? For many students, school shopping just isn't necessary. These students go to school where school uniforms are required. School uniforms are typically a white shirt with dark pants or a skirt. There is no need to check out the local ads for the new styles or trends—these children already know what they will wear on the first day of school long before it arrives.

Some people feel that uniforms are not a good idea. They think that children should be able to have a choice in what they wear. Wearing uniforms seems too strict. Bad behavior doesn't happen because of the clothes they are wearing. Uniforms can be a hassle. Some people feel that they are uncomfortable. It can be boring to wear the same thing every day.

On the other hand, many people agree with student uniforms. These people feel that uniforms make all students feel safe and comfortable. You don't have to worry about gangs when everyone is wearing the same uniform. Behavior improves when students wear a uniform and dress nicely. Uniforms can also be much cheaper than the latest fads. Some say that uniforms are easy to wear, and they are comfortable, too.

So what is your opinion?

## STORY QUESTIONS

1. What is the main idea of the third paragraph about school uniforms?
   a. School uniforms may be a good idea.
   b. School uniforms show school spirit.
   c. School uniforms can be expensive.
   d. School uniforms are uncomfortable, but they keep the students in line.

2. What is one of the reasons presented in the passage that supports the idea that student uniforms improve student behavior?
   a. Students are more comfortable in school uniforms.
   b. There are winter and summer uniforms available.
   c. Students can't wear gang-related clothing if school uniforms are the rule.
   d. Students feel safe at school because the uniforms are protective gear.

3. Which statement shows that the author is trying to appeal to the parents in the audience?
   a. Wearing uniforms seems too strict.
   b. Uniforms can be much cheaper than the latest fads.
   c. Uniforms are easy to wear and comfortable.
   d. Uniforms can be a hassle.

# ENOUGH SLEEP

Yawn! Are you getting enough sleep? There are experts who don't think you are. The average bedtime for most children today is much later than it used to be. Years ago, children used to go to bed by 7:30 P.M. Today, children are lucky to get in bed by 9:00 P.M. There are many reasons why experts believe this is the case.

One of the reasons is because children are involved in too many activities. Children have the opportunity to be involved in soccer, ballet, basketball, ceramics, Girl Scouts, football, piano, and more. There is no end to the number of activities in which children can become involved. This means that as soon as school is out, many children are expected to attend practices. By the time children get home, they get a quick bite of dinner to eat. After dinner, there needs to be time set aside to complete homework. Most children want to watch some television before they take a bath or shower and get to bed.

Another reason children aren't sleeping as much is because more and more families have both parents working. By the time parents get home, they have a lot of work to do. They need to get dinner going. They need to run children here and there. And they need to help children with homework.

Families need to cut back. Children need to be involved in fewer activities. Parents need to come up with a better schedule for the family. Children need more sleep!

## STORY QUESTIONS

1. What is meant by the phrase *cut back* in the passage?
   a. budgets are being reduced
   b. pulling away
   c. reduce and simplify
   d. eliminate activities

2. Which of the following statements is <u>not</u> one of the reasons kids don't get enough sleep?
   a. Children are involved in too many activities.
   b. Both parents are working and there isn't enough time.
   c. Children are busy attending practices and doing homework.
   d. Children have to be at school too early in the morning.

3. Which words best describe the children mentioned in this passage?
   a. harried and worn out
   b. prepared and adjusted
   c. calm and peaceful
   d. chaotic and smooth

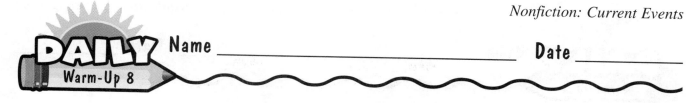

Name _____    Date _____

# AMOUNT OF HOMEWORK

Did you get your homework done last night? Do you feel you have enough homework, or do you feel that you have too much? This has been an argument that has been going on for years. Teachers and parents have differing opinions on the matter. Some teachers feel that a lot of homework should go home. On the other hand, some parents feel that there is not enough or just too much homework coming home! How much is enough?

Many experts believe that some homework should go home, but they don't all agree about the amounts. Experts also say that homework should be for review only. This means that a teacher shouldn't send home anything that is new. A student should only practice and complete work that has been taught in school. It can be confusing for a student to do new material alone.

Experts also say that teachers should only send homework that students can do without any parental assistance. Too many times, teachers send homework that requires an adult to assist in completing it. This is too demanding on the families. Teachers should never send homework just for fun. Homework should always be meaningful and helpful. So, what are your thoughts? Do you agree with the experts? What type of homework do you have? Is it the right kind and right amount?

## STORY QUESTIONS

1. What is the main idea of this passage?
   a. The type and amount of homework should be reasonable.
   b. There is not enough homework going home.
   c. Homework can be time-consuming for the family.
   d. Experts disagree on the amount of homework that is sent home.

2. Who is the audience for this reading passage?
   a. school experts
   b. teachers
   c. parents
   d. students

3. Which statement from the reading passage shows who is the audience for this passage?
   a. Experts say that teachers should only send home work that students can do on their own.
   b. Homework should always be meaningful activities.
   c. Did you get your homework done last night?
   d. Homework should never be something new.

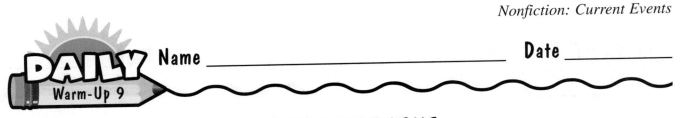

Name _____     Date _____

# HEAVY BACKPACKS

Do you carry a backpack to school each day?  How heavy is the backpack?  Some experts believe that the backpacks that students carry are too heavy.  It isn't because books are heavier these days.  Rather, experts say that students are expected to carry more and more books in their backpacks.  These books are heavy and cause a strain on the students' backs.

Experts say that the backpack should not weigh more than 10–15% of a student's body weight.  Anything heavier than that can lead to back problems.  The problems range from muscle strain to poor back alignment.  The number of people being treated for backpack strain has increased.  Emergency rooms are noticing a rise in the problem.

Does carrying a backpack that is too heavy really cause a problem?  Apparently it does.  Some of the signs to watch for are if the student complains of back pain or if he or she walks bent over sideways to adjust for the weight.  Another sign to watch for is if they complain of tingling in the arms or hands.

To accommodate for the weight, experts recommend that students bring a backpack to school that has wheels.  Another recommendation is a backpack with a waist strap.  The strap helps to support the waist.

## STORY QUESTIONS

1. "To *accommodate* for the weight, experts recommend that students bring a backpack to school that has wheels." *Accommodate* means . . .
   a. to make room for.
   b. to show strength for.
   c. to compensate or adjust for.
   d. to rely on.

2. Why are the backpacks that students carry heavier these days?
   a. Students are more comfortable with the amount of homework assigned.
   b. Students are expected to carry more books around.
   c. Students risk muscle strain or poor back alignment.
   d. Students are assigned more homework these days.

3. The passage is mostly about . . .
   a. learning to use a backpack correctly.
   b. bringing less books in your backpack.
   c. being aware of the weight you carry around in your backpack.
   d. knowing the signs of back pain and muscle strain.

**Name** _____ **Date** _____

# CELL PHONES

Cell phones are not allowed at most schools, but not all students are happy about this fact. There are two sides to the issue. Some feel that cell phones at school are distracting and are not necessary. Others feel that having access to a cell phone is a must.

Many parents give their children a cell phone so that they can have immediate contact. With more and more violence occurring at school, parents want to know that their children are safe.

Those on this side of the issue also believe that students should keep the cell phone on vibrate to prevent interruptions. This group understands that students may not be able to immediately answer a phone call because they may be in the middle of a test or a lecture.

On the other side of the issue, there are those who feel that cell phones should not be allowed at schools. There is no reason that parents need to be able to contact their children during school hours. Parents have always been able to check in with the school if they need to communicate with their children.

Cell phones also add to the problem of cheating in school. If students have access to their cell phones during school, they are able to send text messages back and forth to other students. A student could text message the answers to test problems to another student.

## STORY QUESTIONS

1. This passage is mostly about . . .
   a. how cell phones disturb the learning at school.
   b. using the cell phone appropriately at school.
   c. learning to eliminate cheating with the cell phone.
   d. whether or not cell phones should be allowed at school.

2. Which of the following statements is a reason why some people would want to have access to a cell phone at school?
   a. to allow students to use the cell phone during a test
   b. to occupy students during recess
   c. to contact students/parents in an emergency
   d. Text messaging at school can save paper.

3. The passage says that cell phones add to the problem of cheating at school. Which sentence supports that statement?
   a. There are those who feel that cell phones should not be allowed at schools.
   b. Parents have always been able to check in with their children at school.
   c. Not all students have cell phones, so text messaging wouldn't be fair.
   d. A student could text message the answers to test problems to another student.

**DAILY** Warm-Up 11

# SCHOOL LUNCH MENU

School lunches have never been known for their quality and taste, but things have gotten even worse. The school lunches that students are expected to eat not only taste bad, but they are unhealthy.

For many students, the school lunch is the only chance they have for a well-balanced meal. But most school lunches are anything but healthy. Most school lunches do not meet the minimum standards for protein, vitamins, calcium, or iron. Most school lunches, however, have more than the suggested amount of fat.

There are things parents can do to help their children make better choices at lunchtime. One way is to look over the lunch menu at home before any choices are made. Discuss choices together. Parents can suggest healthier choices. If there are no healthy choices available, then parents can suggest a lunch from home. Parents can teach children to avoid chips, sodas, and sweets.

One of the best ways that parents can teach children how to eat healthy is to set a good example. The family eating habits at home often follow the student to school. If the student is used to eating unhealthy meals, then the same habits will take place during lunchtime at school.

## STORY QUESTIONS

**1.** What is the main idea of the third paragraph?
   a. Money should be set aside in the school budget for healthier lunches.
   b. Parents should discuss healthy lunch choices with their child.
   c. Sending lunch from home is always a healthier choice.
   d. Parents are sharing their eating habits with their children.

**2.** You can infer from the passage that the author feels school lunches should be required to . . .
   a. serve appetizing lunches to the students.
   b. meet minimum standards for protein, vitamins, calcium, and iron.
   c. help children make better food choices.
   d. set the standards for parents to follow at home.

**3.** What does the author say will happen if the student is used to eating unhealthy meals at home?
   a. The student will have the same eating habits at school.
   b. Parents will change their habits of eating at home.
   c. The lunch menu will be more closely observed.
   d. School lunches have less fat in them.

# QUALITY OF CHILDREN'S MOVIES

Since the beginning of animation, movie producers have used animated movies to entertain children and adults alike. But lately it seems like that is all that's offered to children. Studios spend lots of money making movies for adults, but little money is spent on making real movies for children—real movies with real people.

When children read a book, they are taken to another place. A book helps the reader experience new things in life through the eyes of a character. Lessons are learned, and children gain from these experiences. These same things can happen with real movies. But what can be learned from an animated movie with a make-believe character or animal? How can children relate to the make-believe setting? Most of these movies have little to offer except for a few laughs.

It seems another goal of these movies is to make money. Pajamas, toys, food, games, and a variety of other items are sold with the pictures of characters on them.

Bring back movies with substance. Bring back the characters with values. Provide children with entertainment that inspires and enlightens. There are more than enough animated movies to last a lifetime. Let's create movies that inspire for a lifetime.

## STORY QUESTIONS

1. What is the author's opinion of animated movies?
   a. Animated movies are shallow and do not inspire.
   b. Animated movies are funny and entertaining.
   c. Animated movies are an inexpensive way to make a movie.
   d. Animated movies are amazing creations.

2. Which statement in the passage portrays the author's opinion?
   a. Pajamas, toys, food, and games are sold with characters from animated movies.
   b. Animated movies take place in a make-believe setting.
   c. Studios spend a lot of money making movies for adults.
   d. Animated movies have little to offer except for a few laughs.

3. What does the statement "Let's create movies that will inspire for a lifetime" mean?
   a. The author wants movies to be shown for a lifetime.
   b. Movies with value and substance can have an impact that lasts for a lifetime.
   c. Movies should be re-run for many years to come.
   d. Movies should be shown to each generation.

**Name** _____  **Date** _____

# EXTRACURRICULAR ACTIVITIES

Can children be involved in too many activities? Some people believe they are. Some experts say that kids are overworked and overstimulated. They feel that students do not have enough time to be kids.

One of the reasons for this is because there are so many choices available. Children can be involved in activities any hour of the day and any day of the year.

How should parents decide how many activities are the right amount? Experts say that parents should set aside time for homework, time to eat dinner as a family, and time for kids to be kids. This means that kids are allowed free time. If these three criteria are met, then extra activities outside of this are considered okay.

Parents should listen closely to their children as well. Children give signals to their parents all the time about how they are doing. Children who are tired all of the time or are struggling with school may need to have their schedules examined and rearranged.

Children may not state their feelings, but they will send messages to parents letting them know how they are feeling about their life. It takes a strong parent to step back and reevaluate how children spend their time.

## STORY QUESTIONS

1. What are the criteria suggested by experts for balancing extracurricular activities?
   a. Kids are allowed free time and money.
   b. There is time for homework, dinner as a family, and free time.
   c. There is time for one extra curricular activity.
   d. The family needs to organize a calendar to keep track of all the activities

2. What type of parents do experts say are the ones who are able to keep their child's life balanced?
   a. dedicated
   b. ambitious
   c. organized
   d. strong

3. Which of the following is <u>not</u> an example of a signal that a child uses to show he or she is "overbooked"?
   a. The child acts tired all the time.
   b. The child feels excited about participating in an activity.
   c. The child feels like they don't have time to eat as a family.
   d. The child is not doing well in school.

**Name** _____ **Date** _____

Warp-Up 14

# DISCIPLINE AT SCHOOL

Think of the behavior of the students at your school. How do students behave? Do they show respect for teachers and leaders? Do teachers follow up on discipline? Are students respectful of themselves and other students? Is there room for improvement at your school?

Violence is becoming a serious problem in schools today. Experts believe that strict rules and procedures are the only way to curb this violence. But this is not what seems to be happening. Many schools seem to be loosening up the accountability they place on their students. In previous years whatever the school said was the law.

Today, parents can come in and complain about how their child is being treated. Parents get their children out of all kinds of situations, only to find that the child repeats the poor behavior. These kinds of parents are, in effect, lessening the security of the school. Children who do not feel there are any boundaries take risks that are unsafe and disrespectful.

Parents need to support the teacher and leaders at school better. Parents need to teach their children that the school rules and expectations should be followed. Teachers should not be afraid to discipline students and follow through on consequences. Violence at school begins with how adults respond to inappropriate student behavior.

## STORY QUESTIONS

1. You can tell from the passage that the author feels that poor discipline at school leads to . . .
   a. less control from parents at school.
   b. security issues at school.
   c. stronger teachers and administration.
   d. confident teachers and students.

2. Which statement from the passage portrays the author's opinion about how to curb violence at school?
   a. Violence is becoming a serious problem in schools today.
   b. Violence at school begins with how adults respond to inappropriate behavior.
   c. Violence at school begins at home.
   d. Children who do not feel there are any boundaries take risks that are unsafe and disrespectful.

3. What is meant by the phrase *loosening up?*
   a. letting go
   b. being more strict
   c. being less strict about rules
   d. designing new rules

Name _____     Date _____

# DRUG-PREVENTION PROGRAMS

There are many programs that have been set up to help keep kids off drugs. The question is whether or not these programs really work. Once a week, time is set aside to allow police officers and teachers to teach these programs. Time is taken away from the important topics and subjects to teach these programs.

It's not that teaching kids to say no to drugs isn't important. The problem is that sitting in a program like this doesn't really change whether or not a child tries drugs.

Research has shown that the most effective way to teach kids not to take drugs comes from the home. Conversations that parents have with their children are more powerful than a quick lesson in class.

There is so much money that is wasted in these programs. Parents need to take back the responsibility. The school needs to get back in the business of teaching math, reading, and writing skills.

## STORY QUESTIONS

1. What is the main idea of the reading passage?
   a. The government is not spending enough money on drug-prevention.
   b. The money for these programs should be given to the parents to teach their children about drugs.
   c. More time needs to be set aside for the drug-prevention programs.
   d. Parents should be responsible to teach their children about drug-prevention, not schools.

2. You can tell from the passage that the author . . .
   a. believes that drug-prevention programs are a waste of money.
   b. believes that drug-prevention programs need to be restructured.
   c. believes that parents should not be responsible for teaching their children about drugs.
   d. believes that drug-prevention programs need better funding.

3. Which of the following statements does <u>not</u> support the author's opinion?
   a. Parents are the best drug-prevention program.
   b. Money for drug programs should be increased.
   c. It is very important to teach children about the effects of drugs.
   d. Sitting in an hour class each week has no effect on drug use and experimentation.

# FICTION

# PROBLEM SOLVED!

Once there was an old man. He had a rooster that crowed every morning. The neighbors did not like this, so they came to visit the old man. They talked to him about his rooster. They asked the old man if he could get his rooster to be quiet. The old man replied that he couldn't get rid of the rooster, but he promised to fix the situation within a week.

The following morning, the rooster crowed, and a donkey was braying. It was very loud. The neighbors came straight to the old man and complained. The old man reminded them that he promised quiet in a week. The neighbors went back home.

The next morning, the rooster, the donkey, and a cow made a lot of noise. The cow could moo as loud as the donkey could bray and the rooster could crow. These loud noises woke all the neighbors up. They complained bitterly to one another.

This continued each day for a week. Each morning a new animal would join the noise. The noise grew louder and louder. By the end of the week, the neighbors marched to the old man and demanded that he fix the noise. The old man promised that all would be quiet in the morning.

The following morning, only the rooster remained. He crowed just once. The neighbors couldn't believe it! The morning was so peaceful and calm. They went to thank the old man for his kindness.

## STORY QUESTIONS

1. How did the old man solve the situation?
   a. He got rid of the rooster.
   b. He added many more animals to his farm.
   c. He created more noise so that the rooster's crowing didn't seem so loud.
   d. He got rid of all of his animals.

2. What can you learn about the old man in this story?
   a. He took pity on his neighbors.
   b. He is very good with animals.
   c. He is tricky and creative when it comes to problem-solving.
   d. He looks out for his neighbors by taking care of their needs right away?

3. Which of the following statements is <u>not</u> true?
   a. The neighbors realized that the problem was never really fixed.
   b. The neighbors complained bitterly to the old man.
   c. The old man added a new animal to the mix every day.
   d. The animals were much too noisy.

Name _____   Date _____

# THE RACE OF THE WOLVES

There once were two wolves named Sam and Seneca. Sam and Seneca did everything together. They would race around the forest, competing against each other constantly. One day Sam was racing as fast he could to get across the forest before Seneca. He dug his heels into the dirt and was as fast as the speed of lightning. Seneca was not far behind. She was mad that she was behind. She was growling as she ran. But alas, Sam won the race.

The following morning, the two challenged each other to another race. Seneca was not about to let Sam beat her this time. So she got up early and did a practice run. When the time of the race came, she felt fit and ready. A bird in the tree sounded the start of the race and the two were off. They were flying through the forest at dizzying speeds. For the first time, Seneca was outrunning Sam. She was gaining more speed as they raced, and Sam was getting upset.

Up ahead on the trail was a family of quails. The proud parents were taking their little babies out for their first walk. They had no idea of the thunder and pounding just moments away.

As the wolves rounded the bend, Seneca could see the covey of quail. For a split second she chose to ignore them, but she could not. She skidded to a stop just in the nick of time. Sam came close behind her. He did not stop. He saw this as his chance to sail past Seneca. He narrowly missed the last little quail. At the end of the race, Sam questioned Seneca as to why she stopped. She confidently replied, "It's better to be safe than sorry."

## STORY QUESTIONS

1. What is a "covey" of quail?
   a. small group or family
   b. organization
   c. mass
   d. hierarchy

2. How is Seneca's behavior an example of how it's better to be safe than sorry?

   _____

   _____

3. Which sentence shows that an accident was likely to occur?
   a. They were flying through the forest at dizzying speeds.
   b. He narrowly missed the last little quail.
   c. She was gaining more speed as they raced and Sam was getting upset.
   d. The proud parents were taking their little babies out for their first walk.

# GOOD AIM

Frederick was the greatest shooter in the land. He was admired for his talent. He shot a bow and arrow with excellent skill. His father was amazed with his young boy. The entire village was impressed.

Each night Frederick would bring home food for dinner. He would shoot birds and wild game. On occasion, he would shoot larger animals. The family and the village were thrilled with his offerings.

Eric was another young man from the village. He too could shoot a bow and arrow, but he was not as good as Frederick. He was angry that he could not shoot as well. He decided to challenge Frederick to a contest. He wanted to be the best in the village.

When the day of the contest finally arrived, the village people gathered around to watch. Eric and Frederick were to shoot at a target. Whoever got the closest to the center would be the winner. Eric would shoot first. As he took his stance, a lion poked his head through the forest. He was looking at Eric. He lunged. Just as Eric went to shoot, Frederick jumped in front of him and shot the lion with an arrow. The lion fell to the ground.

The village people saw what Frederick had done to save Eric. They all cheered. Eric was speechless. He was so grateful that Frederick had saved his life that he dropped his bow and arrow and bowed to Frederick calling him the greatest shooter in the land.

## STORY QUESTIONS

*1.* Which sentence shows that Eric was no longer angry with Frederick?
   a. They were to shoot at a target.
   b. He wanted to be the best in the village.
   c. He dropped his bow and arrow and bowed to Frederick.
   d. He decided to challenge Frederick to a contest.

*2.* What is the meaning of the word *stance* as used in the story?
   a. marksman
   b. turn
   c. posture
   d. arrangement

*3.* Which of the following idioms goes with the story?
   a. Never count your eggs before they hatch.
   b. Don't cry over spilt milk.
   c. Don't bite the hand that feeds you.

Name _____  Date _____

# COOKING FOR TURKEY

There once was a chicken, a duck, and a goose. These three were the best of friends, but their best friend of all was Mr. Turkey.

One morning, Mr. Turkey awoke with the flu. He was sicker than he had ever been. He could barely breathe, and his feathers were all limp. Mr. Turkey's friends knew that he needed help and he needed it fast.

Each friend independently decided to help Mr. Turkey. The goose got a big pot and put it on the fire. She was going to cook a nice broth for Mr. Turkey.

The chicken also wanted to feed Mr. Turkey, but she had it in her mind to make a turnip pie. She was tickled when she saw the pot on the fire and threw her turnips in to boil.

The duck wanted to help Mr. Turkey as well. He came in and saw the pot on the fire and the turnips inside. He decided to add some cinnamon to the pot to make his sugary cinnamon tea. Each friend, in turn, came and added more ingredients to the pot. It wasn't long before Mr. Turkey hobbled into the room.

"What's that awful smell?" he asked. His three friends entered the room with hurt looks on their faces. They couldn't believe what their friend had said—until they too looked in the pot. With a laugh they all said, "I guess it's true. Too many cooks spoil the broth!"

## STORY QUESTIONS

**1.** What does the word *independently* mean in the story?
   a. artistic
   b. separately
   c. thoughtfully
   d. organized

**2.** Which paragraph contains Mr. Turkey's response to the boiling pot?
   a. fifth paragraph
   b. second paragraph
   c. third paragraph
   d. sixth paragraph

**3.** Which of the following would make a good title for the story?
   a. "Caring for Mr. Turkey"
   b. "Turkey, Goose, and Duck"
   c. "House Visit"
   d. "Turkey Tea"

**4.** Which of the following idioms goes with the story?
   a. Never count your eggs before they hatch.
   b. Wash your hands before dinner.
   c. Too many cooks spoil the broth.

# COMING AROUND AGAIN

Once there was a rabbit named Reese. Each day he would jump around and play all day. He never seemed to have a care in the world. His mother had tried and tried to teach him to work hard, but it was to no avail. Reese resisted all efforts.

Reese learned quickly that he was a smooth talker. He could talk himself out of anything, and he could talk others into anything he wanted. One day he talked a younger rabbit out of his meal. The young rabbit had worked all morning putting together a delicious bundle of vegetables. Reese talked him out of his food. The young rabbit hopped off to get a bite to eat. Reese was becoming accustomed to all the rabbits doing what he pleased. But the rabbits were beginning to catch on, and they decided this had to stop. The rabbits devised a plan.

The next morning, the rabbits gathered up their breakfast of carrots and celery. Reese woke up late and hopped over to where the rabbits were working. He sweet-talked the rabbits out of their breakfast again. But this time the rabbits watched and waited. They had picked vegetables that were not yet ripe, and sure enough, an hour or so after eating, Reese had a stomachache. He moaned and groaned. The other rabbits gathered around him and explained that it was no longer acceptable for him to treat them that way. Reese relented and promised never to trick any of the rabbits again.

## STORY QUESTIONS

1. Where in the story is the conflict stated?
   a. second paragraph
   b. end of the first paragraph
   c. end of the third paragraph
   d. beginning of the first paragraph

2. What is the conflict or problem of this story?
   a. Reese doesn't know how to pick his own vegetables.
   b. Reese doesn't like to eat vegetables.
   c. Reese doesn't like to work for his food and instead wants to live off others' work.
   d. Reese has not been taught how to care for himself so he wants others to care for him.

3. What is the meaning of the word *relented* as used in the story?
   a. defense
   b. reworded
   c. decided
   d. give in

4. What is the moral to the story?
   a. Don't judge a book by its cover.
   b. People who live in glass houses shouldn't throw stones.
   c. What goes around, comes around.
   d. A friend in need is a friend indeed.

**Name** _____   **Date** _____

# THE COVER

It was a hot day in the desert when the old tortoise awoke from a nap. A lizard slithered across the sand in front of the tortoise and said, "Have you seen the new tortoise in these parts?"

"I haven't," responded the old tortoise.

"Well, folks say that this new tortoise is quicker than any of you old guys."

"No way," said the old tortoise. "There's a lot to be said for experience."

"I guess we'll find out at the tortoise race tomorrow," said the lizard as he sauntered off.

"Hmm!" said the old tortoise. He wasn't afraid.

The next morning, all of the desert animals gathered to watch the tortoise race. It was the highlight of the year. All of the tortoises lined up along the starting line. The new tortoise poked his head through the grass. He was nervous. Someone hollered for the new tortoise to join them. As he stepped out, a hush fell from the crowd. This tortoise was small with a cracked shell.

"That tortoise is going to be easy to beat," whispered the tortoises. "He's falling apart!"

The young tortoise went to the line. The race began and the tortoises were off. All of the desert animals gathered at the finish line. They were stunned to see the young tortoise reach the finish line first. The crack in his shell did not affect his racing skills. The tortoises couldn't have been more wrong about him. They all agreed that he won the race and gave him a standing ovation.

## STORY QUESTIONS

*1.* What is the moral to the story?
   a. Birds of a feather flock together.
   b. One for all, and all for one.
   c. Work before play.
   d. Don't judge a book by its cover.

*2.* What is the meaning of the word *sauntered*?
   a. poked          c. directed
   b. walked         d. ran

*3.* How do you think the new tortoise was treated after the race?

   _____

   _____

   _____

# FLAMINGO FOIBLES

Freddy the Flamingo's first word was "sorry." He was born apologizing and never seemed to pass a day without doing so. He was sorry for tripping other flamingoes on accident, and he was sorry for accidentally eating someone else's food.

One day Freddy was feeding next to the biggest flamingo in the group. His name was Frank. Frank loved to eat his breakfast under the shade of the water trees. Freddy was busy getting his food. Freddy was humming as he ate, when all of a sudden he saw some flamingo legs standing directly in front of him. He looked up to see Frank staring at him.

"Oh, sorry!" said Freddy. "I didn't know I was in your way!"

"That's okay," said Frank.

"No, really, I'm sorry," insisted Freddy.

"I believe you," said Frank. "Now move on."

"No, no, no," said Freddy. "I don't think you understand!"

Just then a crane swooped down and ate a fish. It startled Freddy so much that he jumped. In jumping, he managed to knock a group of flamingos flat on their backs, including Frank. Freddy immediately jumped up and said, "Oh! I'm sorry. I'm sorry! I did not mean to do this. Oh! Will you ever forgive me?"

Frank slowly rose to his feet and stood directly over Freddy. He spoke in a low, deep voice. "Freddy, I'm only going to say this once: It's okay. Move on. Don't dwell on it!" And with that, Frank sauntered off to find another feeding spot.

## STORY QUESTIONS

1. What is the moral to the story?
   a. What goes around, comes around.
   b. Work before play.
   c. A rolling stone gathers no moss.
   d. No use crying over spilt milk.

2. What could be a different title for this reading passage?
   a. "Move On, Freddy"
   b. "Freddy vs. Frank"
   c. "The Leader of the Pack"
   d. "Feeding Ground Fodder"

3. Which statement below is <u>not</u> true in the story?
   a. Freddy seemed insecure about himself.
   b. Frank disliked Freddy.
   c. Frank gave Freddy a break.
   d. Frank seemed annoyed with Freddy.

**Name** _____    **Date** _____

# HOUSEWORK

Once there was a mother mouse. She was very proud of her five mouse children. The mouse family lived in the house of a human family. The mouse family worked hard to keep the human home clean. After each meal, the mice would scurry out to pick up crumbs and other things that had dropped to the floor.

It was a busy and hectic life, but this was a hard-working mouse family. That is, except for one family member. Mina Mouse was content to spend her days lying around. She had no desire to work and managed to get out of most of the chores.

One day, Mother Mouse knew that things had to change! She sat Mina down and explained that she had to start carrying her own weight.

"But Mother," protested Mina.

"No, my child. You will one day see the wisdom in this," replied Mother Mouse.

And that day was soon to come. The next morning, Mother gave out assignments. The mice children hurried to get their jobs done so that they could play—that is, except for Mina. She spent her morning complaining.

Suddenly there was a knock at the door. Mother answered the door and found her neighbor inviting the children to go with them to the feline circus. Mother allowed all of her children to go as long as their chores were done. Everyone had their chores done . . . except for Mina. From that day forward, Mina always managed to get her jobs done first.

## STORY QUESTIONS

1. What did Mother Mouse mean when she talked to Mina about "carrying her own weight"?

   _____

   _____

   _____

2. What is the meaning of the word *hectic* as used in the story?
   a. chilly                    c. disruptive
   b. frantic                   d  calm

3. What is the moral to this story?
   a. A bird in hand is better than three in a bush.
   b. A friend in need is a friend indeed.
   c. Work before play.

# PRINCESS PROBLEMS

Isabel was a princess. Most girls would have loved to take her place, but Isabel was hopelessly depressed. She despised being a princess. Day in and day out she hated wearing dresses, and she never knew what to do with her ladies-in-waiting.

One day, as she sat in her room, she noticed a frog hopping across the windowsill. She gently opened the window and called to the little frog.

"Mr. Frog, please come back here. I have a question for you," called Isabel.

The frog hopped back to the window where the princess was standing. "Yes?"

"If I kissed you, what would happen? Would you turn into a prince?" asked Isabel.

"No. You would be the one changing. You would turn into whatever you were thinking of."

"That sounds like exactly what I need," replied the princess.

"Yes. But be careful. Many people are not happy with what they change into. They learn they were much happier with the way they were," cautioned the frog.

"Oh, don't worry. I'd like to be just about anyone else right now." Isabel scooped up the frog and puckered her lips. Just then, a dog ran through the garden below. It made Isabel think of her own dog. Before she knew it, Isabel looked down and saw white fur all over her body. She couldn't believe it. What had she done?

The frog shook his head and hopped away saying, "The grass always does look greener."

## STORY QUESTIONS

*1.* What is the problem in the story?
   a. Isabel wants to marry a prince.
   b. Isabel wants to be a different kind of princess.
   c. Isabel wants to be more like her dog.
   d. Isabel no longer wants to be a princess.

*2.* Which of the following words best describes Princess Isabel?
   a. unhappy
   b. insecure
   c. quick-witted
   d. tall

*3.* If she had it to do over again, what do you think Isabel would do?
   a. She would focus harder and think only about what she really wanted to be.
   b. She would take the frog indoors so no animals could run by.
   c. She would find out more information about the frog.
   d. She would not be so trusting.

# FUNNY FRIEDA

Frieda the Fox was one of the young foxes learning how to hunt. She would practice her skills every day. She wanted to be one of the best, but she still had a lot to learn. Her dad took her out one day, and Frieda found a mouse to chase. She chased the mouse and almost caught it, until she saw a rabbit hop by. She stopped chasing the mouse and began chasing the rabbit.

"Silly Frieda. Why did you do that?" asked her dad.

"Dad! A rabbit would have been a bigger and better catch."

Her dad just shook his head.

The next day they went hunting again. Frieda did the same thing except this time she stopped chasing a rabbit to chase a chicken. She came home with neither. When they got back, all of Frieda's brothers and sisters had a catch. Frieda sat by herself in the back and pouted. She almost had the chicken and the rabbit, but instead she came home with neither.

The next day, Frieda went hunting alone. This time she decided that she would catch whatever animal she saw first. There would be no switching gears to go after another animal. It wasn't long before she saw a hen strutting by. She decided this was it. She raced after the hen and made her pounce. It worked! She got the hen. She proudly walked home to show her dad.

He was thrilled, telling Frieda, "Yeah! You finally got it!"

## STORY QUESTIONS

1. What lesson did Frieda finally "get?"
   a. Good things come in small packages.
   b. Birds of a feather flock together.
   c. The early bird gets the worm.
   d. A bird in hand is better than three in the bush.

2. What does the word *strutting* mean?
   a. afraid
   b. slumping
   c. defensive
   d. swaggering

3. Which sentence below is not true?
   a. Frieda is learning to hunt.
   b. Frieda's siblings were able to catch food.
   c. Frieda is tired of listening to her dad.
   d. Frieda exercises patience in her last hunt.

4. Which of the following animals was not in the story?
   a. rat
   b. hen
   c. rabbit
   d. mouse

# EARLY TO RISE

An old man and a boy lived in a hut. The old man had taken the young boy as an apprentice. He was a carpenter, and he trained the boy to make things out of wood. Each morning, they would get supplies in town. They used the supplies to make items to sell.

The old man knew that some day the boy would be left alone. He wanted to teach him all he could, and so one day he decided to send the boy to town for supplies all by himself.

The old man woke the boy up at 5:00 in the morning and sent him on his way. The boy came home with all of his supplies, but he was exhausted. The next morning, he woke the boy up at 5:00 and sent him to town. The boy came home again with all he needed. On the third morning, the old man woke him again at 5:00. The boy wondered why the old man was doing this.

The next morning, the old man did not wake the boy. The boy woke up on his own. He didn't wake up until 8:00 in the morning and he did not get to town until 9:00 A.M. By the time he got to town, there were no supplies left. The wood pile had been picked over. Saddened, the boy returned home with little. He realized the lesson that the old man had been trying to teach him.

## STORY QUESTIONS

1. What happened first?
   a. The boy went to town at 5:00 A.M.
   b. The boy went to town at 9:00 A.M.
   c. The boy is taught to carve wood.
   d. The boy returns home with little.

2. What is the lesson the old man was trying to teach him?
   a. A rolling stone gathers no moss.
   b. What goes around comes around.
   c. Practice makes perfect.
   d. The early bird gets the worm.

3. Which of the following statements is true?
   a. The old man worked the boy too hard.
   b. The boy learned to get up early to get the good stuff.
   c. The boy forgot the day he was to go to town.
   d. The boy did not like living with the old man.

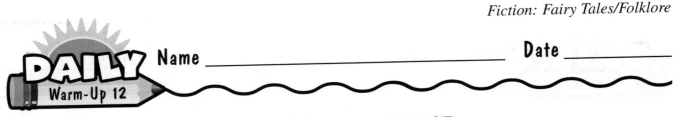

**Name** _____ **Date** _____

# PRACTICING PATIENCE

Two magpies were racing from one tree to another. They loved to chase each other and be the first to get their food. The owl, on the other hand, loved to sit for hours and watch the forest animals. Occasionally he would swoop down to get a bite to eat, but for the most part he was content to sit in a tree.

The magpies thought it was strange that a bird could sit in the tree all day. Didn't he want to be the first to get his meal? The magpies approached the owl and asked, "Mr. Owl, why do you sit in the tree all day and wait for your food to come? Why don't you fly around like us and find your food?"

"I am content to wait for the right time to get my food," replied the owl.

The magpies didn't understand the owl. They thought, "There is no such thing as a right time. You have to hurry if you want to get any food at all." But the owl continued to sit on the limb of the tree and observe from on high while the magpies fluttered around fighting over bites to eat.

On one particular day, the two magpies had not been able to find anything to eat. They were angry and upset. Out of desperation, they decided to try the owl's trick. They sat in the tree and patiently waited for signs of food. Sure enough, the signs came.

## STORY QUESTIONS

1. What is the moral of this story?
   a. What goes around, comes around.
   b. Work before play.
   c. A rolling stone gathers no moss.
   d. Patience is bitter, but its fruit is sweet.

2. What would be a good title for this reading passage?
   a. "Patience Is a Virtue"
   b. "The Two Magpies"
   c. "The Owl"
   d. "Forget the Food"

3. Which statement below is <u>not</u> a fact?
   a. The magpies were always in a hurry to get their food.
   b. The magpies ignored the owl.
   c. The magpies didn't understand why the owl would wait for his food.
   d. The owl taught the magpies the importance of patience.

# SCRAMBLED EGGS

It was common practice for three coyotes to sneak into the farmer's henhouse to steal the eggs at night. Each coyote would bring a basket in which to carry the eggs, except for one. This coyote would bring only one egg home at a time. He made multiple trips back and forth to the henhouse and his den. The other coyotes thought this was quite funny. They made fun of this coyote, calling him a slow poke. "You are a foolish coyote," cried the leader. "Wouldn't it be much easier to make just one trip?"

The coyote ignored the others and continued with his pattern. One night, the farmer got wind of the fact that the coyotes were the ones stealing the eggs. The slow coyote started early in the evening and gathered an egg and returned home. He made two more trips before he saw a light go on in the farmhouse.

The other coyotes were coming by at this time to make their only trip. They quickly loaded their baskets and ran. But it was too late. The farmer chased them, and they dropped all of their baskets. The eggs cracked and broke all over the place.

It was a hungry morning the next day as none of the coyotes had any breakfast—that is, except for the slow coyote. He had plenty of eggs, as he had made plenty of trips. He kindly shared his egg breakfast with the rest of the pack.

## STORY QUESTIONS

1. What is the problem in the story?
   a. The coyotes are trying to get eggs for breakfast.
   b. The farmer breaks the eggs in each basket.
   c. The coyotes that loaded baskets full of eggs lost all of their eggs.
   d. The slow coyote doesn't want to share the eggs.

2. Which of the following words best describes the slow coyote?
   a. smart
   b. insecure
   c. quick-witted
   d. dull

3. What is the moral to the story?
   a. People in glass houses shouldn't throw stones.
   b. Beauty is in the eye of the beholder.
   c. Big things come in small packages.
   d. Don't put all of your eggs in one basket.

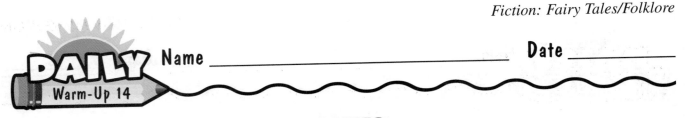

**Name** _____     **Date** _____

# IN NEED

The bear, the wolf, and the wild boar walked together listing all of their friends. They were bragging about who had the most friends. The bear listed the bison, the antelope, and the bighorn sheep. The bear explained all the great qualities that his friends had, and he mentioned the great things he was able to do for his friends.

Not to be outdone, the wolf began listing his friends. His friends included the moose, the deer, and the coyote. The wolf explained the differences between his friends and those of the bear. The wild boar said nothing.

The wolf asked, "Boar, have you no friends?"

The boar did not respond, and the three continued on their walk in the forest. Around the bend, they saw a raccoon that was stuck in a bush. The raccoon was crying and looked like he was in need of help.

The boar asked the bear and the wolf, "Do you know this animal? Is he your friend?"

"No!" the two responded indignantly. "Do you know him, Boar?"

"I do not know him, but he is a friend of mine," replied the boar.

The bear and the wolf looked at him questioningly.

As they approached the raccoon, the boar helped him get free. He dried the raccoon's tears and sent him on his way.

The raccoon responded by saying, "Oh, thank you, Mr. Boar. You are the best friend I have ever had!"

## STORY QUESTIONS

*1.* What was the lesson learned in this story?

    a. Patience is a virtue.

    b. A friend in need is a friend indeed.

    c. People in glass houses shouldn't throw stones.

    d. A watched pot never boils.

*2.* How does Boar teach his lesson?

    a. He contradicts the bear and the wolf.

    b. He takes advantage of the raccoon.

    c. He teaches by example.

    d. He shames the bear and the wolf into helping the raccoon.

*3.* Using the context clues, what is the meaning of the word *indignantly?*

    a. happily

    b. worriedly

    c. angrily

    d. loudly

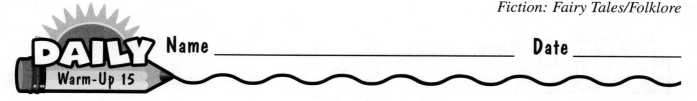

Name _____ Date _____

# PERFECTION

Many in the village knew that Ketu had a hard time singing. They often plugged their ears as he sang. His singing made the babies in the village cry. Many people asked Ketu to stop singing, but he never did. He was sad that he could not sing very well, but he refused to quit singing.

One morning, he awoke to the sound of the birds singing beautiful songs outside of his window. He decided then and there that he would take singing lessons from the birds. Each day Ketu would rise before the sun was awake. He would walk into the forest and sing with the birds. He sang day after day.

One day a ceremony was held in the village. All of the village people were gathered at the ceremony. It was a day of great pride and joy for the village. It was the celebration of their new king.

The new king did not know that Ketu could not sing very well. At the opening of the ceremony, he called on Ketu to sing, and all of the village people moaned and covered their ears. But they were flabbergasted to hear the most beautiful voice singing. They were surprised to see that it was Ketu who was singing so beautifully. They could not believe their ears.

From that day forward, Ketu was always asked to sing at all celebrations and ceremonies. From then on, he was seen as the master singer of the village.

## STORY QUESTIONS

*1.* What is the moral to the story?

   a. Birds of a feather flock together.

   b. One for all, and all for one.

   c. Practice makes perfect.

   d. Don't judge a book by its cover.

*2.* What is the meaning of the word *flabbergasted*?

   a. astonished

   b. annoyed

   c. ignored

   d. ruined

*3.* What lesson do you think the village people learned from Ketu?

_____

_____

_____

# SURPRISING TWIST

The king sent a proclamation to all the land that he was in need of a personal companion. The king needed someone he could trust and someone he could enjoy spending time with.

When the lion came through the door, the king was pleased. He knew the lion would make a great companion. He asked the lion to explain his talents for the king.

The lion responded with, "I am big. I am respected. I can roar loudly. I can be fierce and I can protect you, your majesty."

The king then asked for the next interviewee. A gasp filled the king's chambers when a mouse entered the room. Giggles were heard throughout the room. The lion laughed the loudest.

"Well, well," said the king. "What can you do for me? You are so small."

The mouse cleared his throat and said, "You are right. I am small. But I am a hard worker and I can solve problems."

Just then the king's crown fell from his head and landed under the table. The lion, anxious to show the king his skill, jumped to get the crown for the king. However, the lion could not get his head through the benches. He could not reach the crown.

The mouse waited patiently and then quietly walked under the bench and retrieved the crown. "Here you go, your majesty," said the mouse, proving his point. The king decided that the mouse would be the best choice.

## STORY QUESTIONS

1. What did the king learn from this experience?
   a. Do not put all your eggs in one basket.
   b. Good things come to those who wait.
   c. Good things come in small packages.
   d. Work before play.

2. From reading the story, which of the following words could be used to describe the lion?
   a. poor
   b. intelligent
   c. arrogant
   d. simple

3. Which character is the "surprising twist" in the story?
   a. king
   b. lion
   c. mouse
   d. none of the above

# CIVIL LOVE

Sweat was dripping down Mary's neck. It was the year 1864, and Mary was helping the wounded soldiers as they came into camp. It was the saddest thing she had ever seen. Most of the men were very young. Mary spent countless hours helping and healing. The hours were endless.

As Mary walked towards the back of the room, she quickly smiled at little Elizabeth. Elizabeth sat in the corner watching Mary's every move. She had gotten separated from her family. They were nowhere to be found. Mary had taken her in and cared for her like a daughter. She rocked the girl at night as she cried and cried for her momma. During the day, little Elizabeth was Mary's helper. She ran and got things as quickly as she could. She seemed to anticipate Mary's every need.

"Do you want to help me?" Mary asked the little girl.

"Me?" Elizabeth pointed to herself in surprise.

"Yes, you!" replied Mary. Mary asked Elizabeth to gather cloths to wipe the sweat and blood off the soldiers as they came in. Elizabeth hurried to the task, helping the soldiers.

The next morning the captain came in to say that Elizabeth's mother was found but that she wouldn't be able to arrive for few more days. Elizabeth shouted with glee. She was excited to be back with her mom. But for now, she had work to do.

"Come on, Miss Mary. We have work to do," Elizabeth said.

## STORY QUESTIONS

1. Which sentence contains evidence that the story takes place during the Civil War?
   a. The hours were endless.
   b. It was the year 1864, and Mary was helping the wounded soldiers
   c. The sweat was dripping down Mary's neck.
   d. Most of the men were so young.

2. Which paragraph explains the circumstances in which Mary was living?
   a. first paragraph
   b. second paragraph
   c. fourth paragraph
   d. third paragraph

3. Who is the main character of the story?
   a. Elizabeth's mother
   b. Elizabeth
   c. Mary
   d. Captain

4. What is the meaning of the word *anticipate* as used in the story?
   a. unbiased and disinterested
   b. impressed and appreciative
   c. know in advance
   d. not care for

# WELCOME HOME

Anna lost her mother three years ago. She and her dad had become the best of friends helping one another, so it was a sad day when she found out that her dad needed to go across the ocean to Europe on business. Being on a ship for three weeks was no place for a young lady, he had said. But where would she go? What would she do?

There was no reason to worry. He would send his daughter up to Boston to live with his sister for a month. Where was Boston? How would she get there? Her father explained that Boston was east of New York. She would travel by train. He would take her by horse to the nearest train station. Her Aunt Jody would be waiting for her. How would she know which one was her Aunt Jody? Her dad smiled and explained that it would be hard to miss her. Apparently she talked very loudly and had a gregarious personality.

The day of the trip arrived and Anna was scared. She had never been out of her little town. She would miss the general store and the horses lined up along the sides of the road. The train finally pulled into Boston. Anna wondered where her aunt was.

Just then, she heard a loud voice booming, "Where is my niece Anna? Has anyone seen Anna?"

Anna giggled to herself. This must be her Aunt Jody. "I'm over here," Anna called.

## STORY QUESTIONS

1. Which sentence below does <u>not</u> show that the story takes place in the past?
   a. Anna gathers up her skirts.
   b. Anna buys candy at the general store.
   c. Anna travels by horse and by train.
   d. Anna meets her Aunt Jody at the train station.

2. What is the meaning of the word *gregarious* as used in the story?
   a. excitable
   b. frustrating
   c. timid
   d. outgoing

3. Which of the following statements cannot be inferred from the story?
   a. Anna has an Aunt Jody who lives in Boston.
   b. Aunt Jody is very excited to have Anna stay with them.
   c. Anna's father is traveling to Europe by ship.
   d. Anna is nervous about making the trip to Boston.

Name _____  Date _____

# YOU'RE FIRED

"Melinda."

My eyes opened slowly. I saw Mama smiling down at me. I smiled, and she said, "Hurry up and get dressed so you can feed the chickens." I hated feeding the chickens. It was my worst job. The chickens were a sticky sort.

I touched the ground with my feet and went downstairs to help Mama.

When I came downstairs, I heard Johnny reading Mama the newspaper.

*"Spring of 1837, cotton prices continue to rise. Farmers hoping for a good year. . . ."*

Suddenly, in the middle of reading, there was a loud and unusual squawking from the chickens.

"I wonder what that is," Mama said.

We all ran out to see a stranger chasing the chickens, trying to catch one. When he saw us, he quickly ran off. Johnny ran to catch him with Mama on his heels. I hitched up my dress and ran off after them.

The chickens were squawking and cackling and flapping their wings furiously. Mama, Johnny, and I were yelling our heads off saying, "Stop! Come back here! Wait! Hold your horses!"

Johnny got close enough to grab the strange boy's suspenders and he pulled him back. Over breakfast we tried to figure out what the boy wanted with our chickens. He explained that he was starving. My dad explained to the boy that there was an easier way to get food and offered him a job caring for the chickens. That was the day I was "fired" from that job. It couldn't have been a happier day.

## STORY QUESTIONS

1. Which would be the most logical explanation as to why Melinda's dad offered the job to the boy who tried to steal their chickens?
   a. He wanted the boy to work off the time they had spent chasing him.
   b. He was trying to punish the boy and knew that it was a terrible job.
   c. He was afraid the boy would steal the chickens if he let him go.
   d. In that time period, many people were out of work, and he was trying to help.

2. According to the passage, which sentence shows how Melinda feels about feeding and caring for the chickens?
   a. That was the day I was "fired" from that job.
   b. Over breakfast we tried to figure out what the boy wanted with our chickens.
   c. That was the day I was fired from my job.
   d. I hated feeding the chickens.

3. What did it mean that Melinda was "fired"?
   a. She was fired because she didn't do the job right.
   b. She was not allowed to be around the chickens any more.
   c. She had heard the word before and wanted to try using it.
   d. She used that word to show that the job was taken away from her.

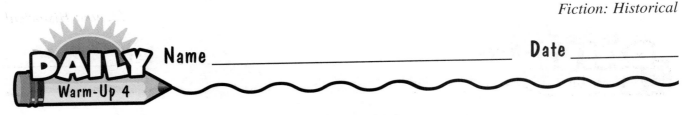

# BABY DOLL

A week before Christmas, Grace and her family made a visit to the general store. It was 1897, and they had lived in the area for two years. Grace loved to travel to town and see all the pretty things in the store. There were dresses, dolls, and lots of candy. She admired all the beautiful things in the storefront window as she waited for her ma and pa to buy the goods.

Grace was enthralled with one of the items in the window that day. It was a baby doll in a beautiful blue dress. She couldn't take her eyes off it. A man standing nearby noticed Grace. He asked her what she was looking at, and she happily pointed it out to the man.

"Looks like you are going to be one lucky girl on Christmas Day."

"Oh no. I won't, sir. You see, my ma and pa, we don't have very much money. We don't get big Christmas presents, but we sure have fun together."

Christmas Day soon arrived. That morning, Grace was surprised to see the little doll from the store window sitting in a cradle under her Christmas tree. Her parents were just as surprised.

"Wow. Santa brought you a real treat, didn't he?" said Pa.

"Oh, this wasn't from Santa. This is from a special man I met at the store," explained Grace with a twinkle in her eye. She smiled when she thought about this stranger who made her Christmas.

## STORY QUESTIONS

*1.* How did Grace know the gift came from the man at the store?

_____

_____

_____

*2.* What does the word *enthralled* mean?
   a. opposite
   b. enchanted
   c. partnership with
   d. opened up

*3.* After reading the passage, what is a word that could be used to describe Grace?
   a. studious
   b. forgetful
   c. gracious
   d. spirited

Name _____     Date _____

# THE GETTYSBURG ADDRESS

On November 19, 1863, President Lincoln had been invited to speak at a dedication of a Civil War cemetery. The Civil War was still in the middle of being fought. Thousands and thousands of soldiers had been killed at Gettysburg, and land had been obtained to bury the dead.

Rebecca had read about the event in a local newspaper. She didn't live far from Gettysburg, and she wanted to go! She begged her parents for a week before they finally relented.

Early on November 19, Rebecca and her father took the quick trip to Gettysburg. She admired Lincoln's bravery and his courage. It had been a dream of hers to one day meet the president. This would be the day.

Rebecca didn't realize how long it would take. Mr. Everett, the first speaker, spoke for two hours. Rebecca thought she was going to die as she sat fidgeting in her seat.

Then it was time for President Lincoln. He rose from his seat and began his speech. Rebecca was enthralled. She loved his words about freedom. President Lincoln spoke for just two minutes. Rebecca couldn't believe it. She jumped out of her seat and ran to the stage. She just had to meet Mr. Lincoln. President Lincoln's bodyguard stopped her, but Mr. Lincoln beckoned her to join him for a minute.

Walking back to the wagon, Rebecca stared at her hand. "I'll never wash it, Dad, never." Her dad smiled and loaded her into the wagon.

## STORY QUESTIONS

1. What was it specifically that Rebecca liked about Mr. Lincoln?
   a. She knew that he would remember her.
   b. She liked him just because he was president.
   c. She liked his words about freedom.
   d. She thought he was nice looking.

2. What is the main idea of the fifth paragraph?
   a. Rebecca was finally able to meet President Lincoln.
   b. Rebecca learned about the Civil War.
   c. Rebecca was planning a trip to Gettysburg.
   d. Rebecca begged her parents for permission.

3. What is the meaning of the word *fidgeting* in the fourth paragraph?
   a. settling                     c. bothering
   b. unconcerning                 d. squirming

Name _____    Date _____

## MAREN'S WISH

The last item was packed in the wagon. Everyone in Maren's family was ready to leave—that is, except for Maren. Maren's dog Missy got lost yesterday. Maren went to bed knowing that if Missy did not show up by morning, she would be left behind. Maren had looked one last time, hoping that Missy was hiding somewhere. But now it was time to go.

That night her family stopped to build a fire for dinner. Maren didn't eat much dinner and was having a hard time getting to sleep. Tears kept coming. Before long, her brother Benjamin called for their pa.

"Pa!" called Ben.

"What is it?" asked Pa.

"I don't know, but it looks like a wolf," he answered.

Maren's heart skipped a beat and she froze with fear. The wolf had probably eaten Missy. Maren's pa grabbed his rifle and stepped outside. He too saw the gleaming eyes in the distance. He knew that if he did not shoot the wolf, it would follow them and try to attack at night.

Maren poked her head out of the wagon. She watched in fear as her pa cocked the gun. Just then she heard a familiar whimper.

"Pa! It's Missy." Maren jumped from her perch and ran to the eyes in the dark. Sure enough, it was Missy. She was a bit bedraggled, but home.

"How on Earth?" asked Pa. A smile crept across Maren's face as she hugged Missy.

## STORY QUESTIONS

1. Which of the following statements is <u>not</u> true in the story?
   a. Missy is Maren's lost dog.
   b. Benjamin hoped that Missy would be shot.
   c. Pa almost shot the dog Missy.
   d. Maren recognizes Missy's whimper just in time.

2. Which of the following words could be used to describe Maren?
   a. angry
   b. devoted
   c. misguided
   d. overly excitable

3. Why does Missy get confused with a wolf in the story?
   a. They both have glowing eyes at night.
   b. The wolf and Missy share the same whimper.
   b. Both animals prowl around at night.
   d. They are both canines.

# THE UNIFORM

Evan climbed to the top of the mountain. He had been with a group of Union soldiers all day. It was his job to get the water and supplies to the soldiers. Evan was young, but he was proud to serve with these men. General Armstead praised his efforts. Evan couldn't wait to wear the uniform one day.

Just then, a messenger rode into camp. The messenger brought word that Confederate soldiers were spotted heading their way. General Armstead signaled the troops to assume their places. It was a hot and sticky day. Evan filled up the water buckets and had them ready.

Before long, shots rang out, and the battle had begun. Evan ran to his place behind the cabin. But it was too late. A stray bullet landed in his leg. Evan shouted out in pain, and a soldier dragged him inside the cabin. The doctor on hand took one look and determined the shrapnel could be pulled easily from his leg. Evan gritted his teeth in pain.

Gunfire soon came to a stop outside. The battle was over for the day. General Armstead came in the cabin and saw Evan sitting with a bandaged leg.

"What happened?" asked the general.

"I got shot," replied Evan sheepishly.

"Well, you better put this on to make it official," said the general as he took off his hat and put it on Evan. Evan smiled through the pain as he touched the piece of the uniform sitting on his head.

## STORY QUESTIONS

*1.* What is the main idea of paragraph three?
   a. Evan is given instructions on caring for the soldiers.
   b. Evan delivers the supplies to the first group.
   c. Evan is planning his future.
   d. Evan is shot in the leg and needs medical attention.

*2.* What did General Armstead mean when he said to wear the hat to make it official?
   a. He wanted Evan to have the same care as a soldier.
   b. He felt that since Evan had been wounded in battle, he'd earned the right to wear the uniform.
   c. He was trying to tease Evan about not having a hat on.
   d. He was sure that if Evan had on a uniform, he would not have been hurt.

*3.* Which of the following did <u>not</u> happen in the story?
   a. Evan was helped by the military doctor.
   b. Evan was able to see his brother fighting for the Union army.
   c. Evan dreamed of being a Union soldier one day.
   d. A messenger brought word on where the enemy was.

# REFUGE FROM THE STORM

Jason had set out on horseback early in the morning. He was intent on finding food for his family. His family was new to the area, having just arrived from Boston. They had a land claim and were beginning their own homestead. It had been a long trip, and the family was exhausted and hungry. Jason knew that a deer or other large animal would bring great satisfaction and relief to his family.

Jason climbed off his horse and crept over the side of the hill. He gazed down the hillside looking for large game. He did not see game, but what he saw was a huge, dark cloud. Jason realized he'd better take shelter quickly. He led his horse to a nearby cave just as the rain came crashing down.

Jason crouched down, waiting for the rain to stop. He worried that he would not have time to catch some food before he had to head back. He had promised to be back before dark. Suddenly he found himself impatient and angry. Why couldn't the rain stop? A cool breeze of wind went down his neck.

Jason heard a noise over his shoulder. He slowly turned to see a large animal staring at him. It was a deer. The deer had gone for shelter too. Jason wasted no time killing the deer and readying it for the trip home. "This is just too good to be true!" thought Jason. At that moment, he didn't mind how long the rainstorm lasted.

## STORY QUESTIONS

1. Which sentence contains evidence that the story takes place in the past?
   a. His family was new to the area having just arrived from Boston.
   b. They had a land claim and were beginning their own homestead.
   c. Suddenly he found himself impatient and angry.
   d. Jason had set out on horseback early in the morning.

2. Which paragraph explains the circumstances in which Jason's family was living?
   a. first paragraph
   b. fourth paragraph
   c. second paragraph
   d. third paragraph

3. What is the meaning of the word *intent* as used in the story?
   a. content and happy
   b. having a goal or purpose
   c. expect and look forward to
   d. rearrange and reconfigure

# SHOT HEARD AROUND THE WORLD

Nathan had been riding his bike outside with friends. It had been a typical day in his life, but he felt unsettled and didn't know why. His favorite team, the Dodgers, had just won the World Series. He waved goodbye to his friend David and wheeled his bike up the steps.

He opened the door and walked inside. He could hear the television playing in the background. His entire family was sitting around the set. He thought it was strange that his dad was home from work so early.

"Hey, what's up?" asked Nathan.

"Oh, Nathan, sit down. Something terrible has happened," replied his mother.

Nathan got a lump in his throat and sat down. What could have happened? Just then, the announcer on the television made the stunning announcement: "We have just received word that President John F. Kennedy has been shot and killed in Dallas, Texas. More information after these commercials."

"President Kennedy shot?" asked Nathan in a stunned voice.

"Yes, just about an hour ago," answered Dad.

Nathan loved President Kennedy. He had been excited to have someone so young in the White House. Nathan realized what this would mean. He ran upstairs to grab his book about the United States. He wanted to know exactly who would become president next.

Nathan read about how the vice president would become president and looked up more information about Lyndon B. Johnson. Nathan wiped his eyes and went downstairs to talk with his family.

## STORY QUESTIONS

1. Which statement from the story shows the year in which the story takes place?
   a. "We have just received word that President John F. Kennedy has been shot and killed in Dallas, Texas."
   b. He ran upstairs to grab his book about the United States.
   c. He could hear the television playing in the background.
   d. His favorite team the, Dodgers, had just won the World Series.

2. What is the meaning of the word *stunned* as used in the story?
   a. excited
   b. bewildered
   c. pressured
   d. coerced

3. Which of the following statements contains information shared in the story?
   a. Nathan's parents voted for President Kennedy.
   b. Lyndon B. Johnson was the vice president when Kennedy was shot.
   c. Nathan had written a letter to President Kennedy.
   d. President Kennedy died of a heart attack.

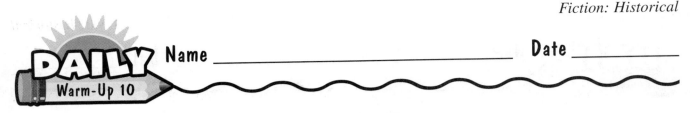

**Name** _____ **Date** _____

# BLAST OFF!

Seth adjusted the straps of his homemade astronaut suit and climbed up the stairs to the treehouse. Seth was an avid astronomer and loved to explore the outer worlds. He had convinced his friend Tim to help him build a spacecraft that would make it to the moon. The boys had spent weeks on the project, but Seth was sure it could be done. Tim wasn't so sure.

The boys had heard about the space race in school. They didn't think that the United States government was doing enough to win the space race, and they were determined to do their part. Tim was upset about the number of days it was taking to put the manifold together. The boys were competitive, and they could feel the intensity of the situation gaining on them.

Just then, Seth's mother called from the house. "Seth Stewart, come here! You have got to see this!"

Seth and Tim hurried down the makeshift ladder and through the door.

Blaring on television was the announcement that Neil Armstrong had just been the first person ever to walk on the moon. Seth and Tim said simultaneously, "Oh, man!"

"It's no use, Seth. It's been done. Someone else beat us to the moon," said Tim.

Seth didn't skip a beat and said, "Come on, Tim. We've got work to do. Let's go try to be the first on Mars."

## STORY QUESTIONS

1. Based on reading the passage, why do you think Seth wanted to go to the moon?
   a. Seth was an avid astronomer and loved to explore the outer worlds.
   b. He wanted to prove to himself that he could do it.
   c. He was afraid no one would ever make it to the moon.
   d. He was inspired by Neil Armstrong.

2. What can you conclude about Seth after reading the passage?
   a. He is friends with everyone.
   b. He shares an interest in the U.S.S.R.
   c. He is competitive and has set high goals.
   d. He is an excellent student in school.

3. Which sentence helps you answer the previous question?
   a. Tim wasn't so sure.
   b. Seth was sure it could be done.
   c. "Let's go try to be the first on Mars."
   d. Blaring on television was the announcement that Neil Armstrong had just been the first person ever to walk on the moon.

# BEING NEEDLED

Lynda hurried upstairs in an intent but deliberate manner. She just had to find her needlepoint. She had it yesterday, but this morning it was nowhere to be found. The ladies from the Society would be over soon. Whatever would she work on? She was excited to share the progress of her needlepoint with the other young ladies.

Lynda checked under her pillow, but the needlepoint was not to be found.

"Lemonade?" asked the maid.

"Not right now, Amelia. I'm trying to find my needlepoint. Have you seen it?" asked Lynda.

"I have not," said Amelia as she put the pitcher back in the refrigerator. "All of the goodies are set for your tea."

"Thank you, Amelia." Lynda scurried upstairs to have one more look. But it was to no avail. The needlepoint could not be found. Just then, the doorbell rang. She heard a group of voices in the hall. Lynda went downstairs with a sad face to greet her guests.

After she welcomed each of the young ladies, she brought them to the sitting room, and Amelia went to get the tea and cookies.

"Whatever is the matter, Lynda?" asked Corrine. "You look as though you have lost your favorite pet."

At that very moment, Lynda sat on the couch. She felt a prick in her leg. She almost let out a cry in pain but giggled instead.

"Oh, nothing, Corrine. I thought I had lost something, but it has been found," smiled Lynda.

## STORY QUESTIONS

*1.* How can you tell that Lynda has found her needlepoint?
   a. Amelia informs her that it is found.
   b. Lynda sees it on the counter in the sitting room.
   c. Lynda accidentally sits on her needlepoint and is poked by the needle.
   d. She has stopped crying.

*2.* What would be a good title for this story?
   a. "Lost for Good"               c. "Needlepoint Instructions"
   b. "Society Tea"                  d. "Needle-less Worries"

*3.* What is another word for *deliberate* as used in this story?
   a. instruction                   c. question
   b. purposeful                    d. gaze

# OVER THE TOP

Franklin and Shiloh set out early in the morning to get the field plowed.  They were brothers and worked well as a team.  Father trusted them to work alone far from home.  These days it was time to plow the fields so they would be ready when the rains came.  Plowing a field was hard work, but not too hard for these two young men.

Old Betsy, the mule, had been teamed and ready.  She did not seem happy about the plans for the day.  Franklin hit her gently on her back, and she began walking.

Halfway through the field, the boys heard a snap and realized that the plow had broken lose from the harness.  The loud snap scared Betsy, and she started to run.  Shiloh ran after Betsy, and Franklin went to survey the damage on the plow.

It was at least 30 minutes before Shiloh came back with Betsy in tow.

"What are we going to do now?" asked Shiloh.

"Well, as far as I can figure," said Franklin, "I've fixed the plow, but it's stuck.  If we can get Betsy to pull it out, I think we're good to go."

The boys harnessed Betsy to the plow and snapped the whip.  Betsy obeyed, but she sent the plow flying.  It sailed right alongside Franklin and Shiloh, who had to jump to get out of the way in time.

"That was close," said Franklin.

"Yes, but we did it," stated Shiloh.  "We did it."

## STORY QUESTIONS

1. What is the main idea of paragraph three?
   a. The plow was finally hitched to Betsy.
   b. The plow broke lose from the harness.
   c. Franklin snapped the whip on Betsy.
   d. Betsy is hit in the leg from the plow and needs medical attention.

2. Which of the following sentences portrays the problem in this story?
   a. Franklin and Shiloh have to work in the heat of the sun.
   b. Shiloh and Franklin have to hurry out of the way of the plow.
   c. Shiloh has to chase after Betsy.
   d. The boys heard a snap and realized that the plow had broken lose.

3. Which of the following did not happen in the story?
   a. Franklin and Shiloh's dad shows up to help.
   b. Franklin devises a plan to fix the plow.
   c. Shiloh chases after Betsy when she got lose.
   d. Franklin and Shiloh work well together as a team.

# SACRIFICE BRINGS BLESSINGS

Jarom came in from school feeling hot and tired. He sure could go for some butter cookies. It had been a long time since he had eaten butter. Just the sound of the word made his mouth water.

Jarom's father was away at war in Europe. He was a military doctor working to help the wounded soldiers in the war. Jarom's family had sacrificed great things—just like many others in the country—to help the men fighting the war.

Jarom looked out the window and saw his mother in the victory garden. She worked daily in the garden. It seemed to keep her mind off things.

They hadn't received a letter from his dad for almost a month. The officer Jarom's mother spoke with assured her that it wasn't uncommon to go through a dry spell without letters or correspondence. That's because he didn't know Jarom's dad. Jarom's dad faithfully wrote a letter each week. Jarom went out to pull weeds with his mom.

"Hi, Jarom. I hope it was a good day," said his mom.

"Good as ever," replied Jarom. Just then, the mailman came up the street. "I have a deal for you, Mom," said Jarom as he tried to cheer his mom up.

"What's that?" asked Mom.

"If a letter comes in the mail from Dad, I'll do the dishes for a week," offered Jarom.

"It's a deal," said Mom. Jarom groaned as he saw the huge smile on the postman's face. He had spoken too soon.

## STORY QUESTIONS

1. Which would be the most logical explanation as to why Jarom's dad didn't write for weeks?
   a. He was tired of writing and it made him homesick.
   b. He just did not have the interest in doing so.
   c. He was afraid his letters were worrying his family.
   d. He had been injured in the war.

2. According to the passage, which sentence shows how Jarom feels about washing the dishes?
   a. Jarom went out to pull weeds with his mom.
   b. Jarom groaned as he saw the huge smile on the postman's face.
   c. "If a letter comes in the mail from dad, I'll do the dishes for a week."
   d. He had spoken too soon.

3. Using the context clues, what is the meaning of the word *correspondence?*
   a. facts
   b. communication
   c. instructions
   d. information

## SICK OF IT

Laura's baby brother was gravely ill. The doctor had been sent for, but it would take at least two days for him to arrive. Laura's family didn't know if her brother would make it that long. Laura had dreamed for many years of having a little sibling. It just didn't seem right to have him taken away so quickly. Little Owen had pneumonia. The disease had stricken many people in town, but it was especially hard on the young and old ones. Owen's cough made the windows rattle. Laura was scared.

Laura was a dutiful sister and sat right by his side morning and night. She kept the water bowl clean and filled. As she slept by his side at night, she would sing lullabies to help him sleep.

"When will the doctor come?" thought Laura.

Early the next morning, Laura was awakened to hear footsteps outside her door. It was the doctor. Laura rose from her chair in the bedroom and hurried to the door. The doctor rushed in with his bag. He quickly unloaded his tools and checked Owen's chest. Owen let out a little cough and smiled at Laura.

"What do you think?" Laura's mother anxiously asked the doctor.

"I think he's going to make it," said the doctor with a twinkle in his eye. "I think he has had the perfect care. I can tell he's got a mother that knows what to do and the devotion of a sister that carried him through."

The doctor left medicine with Laura's mother, and Laura sat down to breathe a huge sigh of relief.

## STORY QUESTIONS

1. Which sentence shows the time period in which the story was written?
   a. Laura's baby brother was gravely ill.
   b. The doctor left medicine with Laura's mother.
   c. He quickly unloaded his tools and checked Owen's chest.
   d. The doctor had been sent for, but it would take at least two days for him to arrive.

2. What conclusions can be drawn about how Owen feels about Laura?
   a. He doesn't know her very well.
   b. He is too sick to care about Laura.
   c. Owen loves Laura as much as she loves him.
   d. Owen is just beginning to learn who Laura is.

3. After reading the passage, which of the following statements helps you answer the previous question?
   a. Owen let out a little cough and smiled at Laura.
   b. Little Owen had pneumonia.
   c. "When will the doctor come?" thought Laura.
   d. Owen's cough made the windows rattle.

# OUT OF THE DUST

Hannah let another tear drop on her pillow that night. She knew she had better stop or else she would have mud all over herself. This wasn't a joke; she was serious. Hannah and her family were living in Oklahoma during the time of the Dust Bowl. Hannah's father had been a farmer, but now he was just like the others trying to scrape money together to feed his family.

Hannah missed her old life. She missed her life before the dust. The next morning at breakfast, she shared her feelings.

"I'm sick of it!" she demanded. "I'm so tired of wiping dust off of everything."

"We're doing the best we can," encouraged Hannah's mother. "It won't last forever you know."

"What do you miss, Hannah?" asked her father.

"I miss our life. I miss laughing and playing outside without a handkerchief over my face. I miss sleeping in my bed without grains of sand to rub my skin raw. I miss dancing together as a family watching the moon come up."

The family quietly finished their meal contemplating Hannah's words. The day continued as usual, but when Hannah came to dinner that night, things were different. She was surprised to see the fancy dishes. She smelled meat cooking. They hadn't had meat for months. Hannah put her hands over her mouth to see the dandelions in a bowl on the table. Just then, someone tapped her shoulder.

"Would you like to dance?" asked her father.

Hannah smiled and said, "Love to!"

## STORY QUESTIONS

1. Using the context clues, what does the word *scrape* mean?
   a. organize
   b. intensify
   c. gather
   d. chide

2. According to the passage, what did Hannah's family do to help her cope with her problems?
   a. They scolded her for not counting her blessings.
   b. They ignored her comments because they couldn't do anything about it.
   c. Her family made plans to move.
   d. They created a special evening for everyone to enjoy.

3. What is the theme of this story?
   a. If at first you don't succeed, try, try again.
   b. If you try hard enough, you can win.
   c. It's important to knock out your competition.
   d. We may not have it all together, but together we have it all.

# SPELLING BEE

Miranda had studied the words for the spelling bee for two weeks straight. Each class in school was to send a student to participate in the school-wide spelling bee. Miranda had always been a good speller. She just had to make it to the school spelling bee.

"Encourage," said her teacher, "encourage."

"E—n—c—o—u—r—a—g—e."

"That's correct," replied the teacher.

Miranda had made it through another round. The room seemed awfully hot. Her friend Patsy had just spelled a word wrong and had to sit down. Miranda gave her a smile across the room. Now it was just Miranda and Kevin. This was going to be close.

Kevin's word was "accommodate." He surprised Miranda and spelled it right. Miranda was up next, and her word was "obstinate." "The boy was acting obstinate when he wouldn't agree to clean his room." Miranda didn't know what the word meant, but she thought she could spell it. She made it through the first part of the word but had to pause for the ending. "Nate." How would this word be spelled? Would it be "nat?" "Nate?" She just wasn't sure.

Just then a picture of her little cousin Nate flashed into her mind. She was pushing him higher and higher on a swing. Before she could think anymore about it, Miranda blurted out the last part, "N-a-t-e."

"That's correct!" yelled her teacher. Everyone was happy that Miranda spelled the word right. Miranda looked up at the ceiling and said, "Thanks, Nate!"

## STORY QUESTIONS

1. Using the context clues, what does the word *obstinate* mean?

   a. surprised

   b. perplexed

   c. stubborn

   d. ferocious

2. According to the passage, what trick helped Miranda spell the word correctly?

   a. She remembered reading the word in a book.

   b. Someone had missed the word right before she had.

   c. Her teacher had helped her practice for the test.

   d. She remembered how to spell her cousin's name.

3. What is the main idea of the passage?

   a. Being creative and using many resources can help you accomplish a task.

   b. If you try hard enough, you can win.

   c. It's important to knock out your competition.

   d. Having a large family can be helpful at times.

# BAKE-SALE BLUES

Jesse, Milo, and Heidy had been planning all week to have a bake sale on Saturday. They had been so excited for the big day to arrive. Saturday arrived before they knew it. The table was ready. Jesse showed up bright and early with her homemade chocolate chip cookies. They were large cookies. Milo came next and he put his plate of cookies on the table. Heidy came riding up the street on her bike. She had her cookies in the basket of her bike.

They put up their sign and sat back to rake in the profits. Their first customer was four-year-old Sam from next door. He had a dollar to spend. Jesse, Milo, and Heidy unwrapped all the plates so Sam could take a look. To their astonishment, everyone had brought chocolate chip cookies! How were they going to be able to sell a lot of goodies if they were all the same things?

Milo was the first to speak. "What? I can't believe this!"

Jesse said, "I told you guys I was going to make chocolate chip cookies. I didn't know you were all going to copy me."

"Copy you?" replied Heidy. "You just said you were making chocolate cookies."

Milo added, "This is a disaster!"

"Relax," interrupted Sam. "This isn't such a big deal! Just change your sign. Change it to say nuts, oatmeal, or plain."

The three kids looked at each other and grinned. Heidy went inside to a get a marker to change the sign.

## STORY QUESTIONS

1. Which sentence shows how the children feel about the change of plans?
   a. "This isn't such a big deal!"
   b. "I didn't know you were all going to copy me."
   c. "What? I can't believe this!"
   d. The three kids looked at each other and grinned.

2. The second paragraph shares with the reader . . .
   a. how to solve the problem.
   b. what the problem was.
   c. the disagreements between the children.
   d. the relationship between the children.

3. Why is Sam's idea a good one?
   a. It makes the best of the situation.
   b. They will be able to save all the cookies.
   c. Sam always has good ideas.

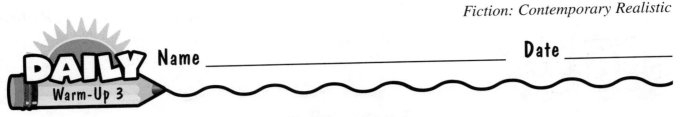

Name _____ Date _____

# OVERBOARD!

Joe sat facing his father in the boat. He was 10 years old and proud of it. He had been in this boat a thousand times, but this time it was different. Joe was going to steer the boat on his own. His father felt that, with a little assistance, Joe could do it.

The night before, Joe dreamt of this moment. He could picture it all in his mind. Sparkling blue water lapped the side of the boat. Once in a while, a small fish would jump out of the water. Joe awoke as excited as can be.

Before long, Joe's dad turned the boat off and slid over to the seat next to the steering wheel. It was time. Joe climbed down into the driver's seat and put his hands on the wheel. This was exciting. In the back of the boat, Joe's sister, Gwen, was rolling her eyes. Gwen was older and wiser. She didn't see the point in letting the little kid drive the boat. Gwen knew it would take a while for the driving instruction, and so she dangled her feet over the edge of the boat.

Joe had other plans. He figured he had watched his dad plenty of times. He threw the boat in gear and the boat lurched forward. Joe heard screaming. He turned to see his sister fly off the back of the boat.

## STORY QUESTIONS

1. Which paragraph explains what Joe had done the night before?
   a. first paragraph
   b. last paragraph
   c. third paragraph
   d. second paragraph

2. What inference can you make about how Gwen is going to react after falling in the water?
   a. She is going to be happy for Joe's first ride.
   b. She is going to climb back in the boat and ask what happened.
   c. She is going to yell and scream at Joe.
   d. She is going to yell at her dad for letting Joe come along.

3. What does Joe need to learn about driving a boat?
   a. He's lucky to have a dad willing to let him try.
   b. It's not as easy as it looks.
   c. He has a supportive sister.
   d. He needs to have professional lessons.

**Name** _____

**Date** _____

DAILY Warm-Up 4

# ARTISTIC TALENT

Eli was running down the hall to art class. He loved art, and he had what people said was natural talent. He slowed to a walk as he ran by Mrs. Robinson's classroom. She was always hollering at him to slow down.

Three more doors and he would be there! Eli slid into class and found his seat at the back table. Mr. Jones was sketching on a pad, waiting for all the students to enter. Eli was so excited to finish up the project he had been working on. It was a birthday present for his dad.

As Eli sat down, he glanced at the counter to see his project. What he saw made him gasp for air. Eli and his dad would never forget this birthday present! Eli's project was covered in blue paint. The only way he knew it was his project was because his name was peeking through the paint. Next to the project was a blue can of paint turned over on its side.

Eli ran to the counter and lifted up the can of paint.

## STORY QUESTIONS

1. Why can't Eli believe what happened in the art room?
   a. The art room is always locked.
   b. Mr. Jones thinks that Eli is a great artist.
   c. He had been warned this could happen.
   d. He never dreamed something like this would happen.

2. What conclusions can be drawn about how Eli will react?
   a. Eli will start to laugh.
   b. Eli will yell at Mr. Jones.
   c. Eli will never paint again.
   d. Eli will try to fix the damage.

3. After reading the passage, which of the following statements helps you answer the previous question?
   a. Eli and his dad would never forget this birthday present!
   b. Eli ran to the counter and lifted up the can of paint.
   c. As Eli sat down, he glanced at the counter to see his project.
   d. What he saw made him gasp for air.

4. Why would Eli and his dad never forget this birthday present?
   a. It was a huge accomplishment.
   b. It showed just how talented Eli was.
   c. It would turn out to be different from the original plan.
   d. His dad would never get a birthday present this year.

Name _____     Date _____

# THE FIELD TRIP

Elise got up early in the morning to pack her lunch. She was going on a field trip today, and she could hardly wait. The plan was to go and visit the Great Salt Lake. This lake had no outlet, and was filled with salt. Elise was fascinated by the idea and couldn't wait to see a salty lake.

The bus trip seemed to take forever. They had packed at least 90 students and adults on the bus. The winding curves of the canyon made this bus trip even more difficult than usual. This was almost too much.

At last the bus was driving across the causeway onto Antelope Island. Elise waited impatiently, tapping her foot as she waited for the students to unload. With a plastic container in hand, Elise headed towards the Salt Lake. Her first scoop of water produced plenty of brine shrimp.

"Yes," thought Elise. "This is the life; exploring and discovering things in nature."

Just then, Elise's friend Brooklyn came running up to her. She was asking Elise at the top of her lungs if she had found any brine shrimp yet. Just before she reached Elise, she tripped and fell right into her. The two girls tumbled into the water.

"Gack!" Elise came up sputtering. "Everything is ruined!"

"Oh, no it's not," said Brooklyn. "I just found some brine shrimp."

"You did? Where?" asked Elise.

"On your head!" giggled Brooklyn, and the girls fell back into the water.

## STORY QUESTIONS

1. Which statement best describes Elise's personality?
   a. Elise is lazy and tired most of the time.
   b. Elise is curious and likes to explore.
   c. Elise is timid, shy, and introverted.
   d. Elise has little interest in school.

2. Which sentence explains the problem in this story?
   a. The two girls tumbled into the water.
   b. "On your head!"
   c. "I just found some brine shrimp."
   d. Her first scoop of water produced plenty of brine shrimp.

3. What does the word *outlet* mean in paragraph one?
   a. detour
   b. opening
   c. dam
   d. constricted

# A SUDSY DAY

Tom rushed into the house just in time for dinner. His family was sitting around the table quietly eating.

"You're late," said Tom's sister. "As usual," she added.

Tom slumped down into his chair and began loading his plate with potatoes. He could hardly wait to tell his parents about his day. It had been most unusual. He was starting to realize that there was a theme.

He started by explaining about how he ran out of soap in the shower this morning. Dripping wet, he managed to get to the cabinet and get some more. Then, in his first period class, he had done a science experiment with soap and vegetable oil. It only got better.

At lunchtime, he heard his friend say a bad word. The teacher washed his mouth out with soap. By this time, Tom was laughing as he recounted his day. His parents smiled. His sister ignored his comments and reminded him it was his turn to load the dishwasher.

After dinner, Tom loaded the dishwasher and turned it on. He left the kitchen and ran up stairs. He didn't make it to the fifth step before his sister screamed at him.

"What?" thought Tom. Walking into the kitchen was like walking onto another planet. Large bubbles covered the floor and floated in the air. His sister was yelling at him as he ran to turn off the machine. He picked up the soap bottle and read, "Dish soap. Not for dishwasher use."

## STORY QUESTIONS

1. What is the theme that Tom refers to in the story?
   a. How crazy things happened to him all day
   b. That everything he did that day had to do with soap
   c. That his sister kept getting upset for no reason at all
   d. That his parents were consistently patient with him

2. What is the meaning of the word *recounted* as used in the story?
   a. directions
   b. ignored
   c. exaggerated
   d. narrated

3. Which word would best describe the sister's feelings?
   a. patient                          c. insistent
   b. annoyed                          d. jolly

DAILY Warm-Up 7

Name _____   Date _____

# THE FIELD DAY

It was a tradition to spend the last day of school participating in a "field day." Eric had been picked to be the anchor of the boys' relay. He couldn't imagine why he was picked for that position. Just the thought of it made him sick.

The long jumpers were busy at work, running, jumping, falling, and laughing. Eric wondered why he couldn't do a simple event like that. There didn't seem to be an ounce of pressure. He took another walk around the track to calm down.

Before long, it was time to race. Eric met with his team and began stretching out. He was so nervous that he thought he would be sick. After stretching, Eric jogged a casual lap around the track. The announcer called for the runners, and Eric's team found their places on the track.

Moments later, the announcer's gun fired into the air. The race was on. Zoom! The racers flew around the track. One of Eric's teammates was racing towards him with the baton.

Eric grasped the baton tightly in his grip and raced toward the finish line. He could feel sweat spraying off of his forehead. Was he going to make it? Before Eric knew what the result was, he was scooped up into the air on his teammates' shoulders. They had done it! Eric smiled and happened to glance over at the long jumpers. He couldn't believe the thought that came to his mind. He thought, "That looks awfully boring."

## STORY QUESTIONS

*1.* Based on reading the passage, why do you think Eric wanted to long jump?
   a. It looked like an event without much pressure.
   b. He was afraid that he was going to get injured.
   c. He was scared to do the high jump.
   d. He didn't have confidence in his teammates.

*2.* What can you conclude about Eric after reading the passage?
   a. He was loved and adored by everyone.
   b. He is a good sport.
   c. He was learning to do the long jump.
   d. He was a great sprinter in the school.

*3.* Which sentence helps you answer the previous question?
   a. Eric jogged a casual lap around the track.
   b. Ben was racing towards him with the baton.
   c. Eric thought his stomach would fall out of his mouth.
   d. Eric had been picked to be the anchor of the boys' relay.

DAILY
Warm-Up 8

Name _____

Date _____

# FAMILY REUNION

"What time is it?"

"It's almost four o'clock."

"What time does the plane get in?"

"Four-thirty."

Brenda said, "Oh, good. They should be here any minute now." It had been an exciting week in Brenda's family. Brenda was 10 years old and an only child. Her parents had tried for years to have more children, but they had been unable to.

For the last two years, they had been working to adopt two children from China. The children were a set of twin girls. Word had finally been received that the time was right. Brenda's mom and grandmother had traveled to pick up the girls and bring them home. Brenda couldn't wait to meet her new sisters.

Brenda's dad stood peering out the window of the airport. Brenda could tell he was nervous because of the way he kept shifting his feet.

"Are you nervous, Dad?" asked Brenda. "It's going to be okay!"

"I know," replied her dad. "I'm just wondering what our house is going to be like with so many girls in it."

Brenda chuckled and gave her dad a hug. Just then, the flight attendant opened the door to the airplane. Brenda stood up on a chair to peer over the crowd.

## STORY QUESTIONS

1. How can you tell that Brenda is comfortable with her parents adopting these children?
   a. She is trying to comfort her dad by telling him it will be okay.
   b. She is concerned about having new kids in the house.
   c. She is expressing concern about what life is going to be like.
   d. She is wishing that her parents would adopt boys instead of girls.

2. What would be a good title for this story?
   a. "Changes"
   b. "Family Additions"
   c. "Girl Concern"
   d. "Process of Adoption"

3. What is another word for *peer* as used in this story?
   a. friend
   b. listen
   c. question
   d. gaze

**Name** _____     **Date** _____

# HAUNTED HALLOWEEN

It was Halloween, and Miriam wanted to do something different this year. She was tired of going trick-or-treating. She wanted to do something exciting, something that seemed more grown up. Her brother Brett had told her about a haunted house at the top of the hill. Miriam had decided that this would be the Halloween that they checked it out.

Miriam met with her friends Pam and Ellie at exactly 8:00 P.M. They walked uphill towards the house. Miriam led the way slowly up the steps to the old house. The girls pressed the doorbell and took a step back. What if someone answered the door? What if no one did? They tried to gather their courage together.

Miriam jumped as the door opened all by itself. She stared at Pam and Ellie, who looked like a pair of ghosts. The curtains were flowing in the wind. The entryway was covered with dust. Miriam took a step forward.

"Come in," a voice boomed. Miriam was scared. Should she leave now? If she did, her brother would think she was a chicken.

Miriam took another step forward. She was shaking with fear. Just then, the voice shouted, "COME IN!" Miriam jumped! All of a sudden, a figure jumped out. Miriam screamed and ran for the door. Something grabbed her arm.

"Miriam! Stop, it's me!" Brett called.

Miriam whirled around to see her brother laughing. She couldn't believe it! Yes, it had indeed been a different Halloween.

---

## STORY QUESTIONS

1. A likely reason people are fascinated with haunted houses is because . . .
   a. they are scary and unknown.
   b. they are liked by everyone.
   c. they are worth so much money.
   d. they have large mirrors.

2. Another word for *figure* is . . .
   a. person.
   b. form.
   c. shadow.
   d. costume.

3. Which sentence explains the problem in this story?
   a. Miriam took a step forward.
   b. Miriam led the way slowly up the steps to the old house.
   c. Something grabbed her arm.
   d. Should she leave now?

# FRIENDS IN THE MORNING

Samantha was not a morning person. Every morning when her mom called, she'd snuggle down under the blankets for a few more minutes. She would stay there until her mom came to get her. She knew that this annoyed her mom and that her mom would come yell at her, but Samantha felt like the extra minutes of comfort and warmth were well worth it.

Then one morning, Samantha woke up and listened. She wondered what time it was. She figured it must not be time to get up yet, so she snuggled back down under the covers. Silence. Samantha began to wonder why she was awake. She began wondering again what time it was. She flipped off the covers and looked at the clock. It read 7:30. She was going to be late! She jumped out of bed and threw on her clothes. Where was her mom? Why hadn't she woken her up?

Samantha ran downstairs to see her parents sitting at the breakfast table drinking their coffee calmly.

"What's going on?" asked Samantha. "Why didn't you wake me up?"

"Oh, I did," replied her mom. "You just chose to stay in bed."

"Mom, is this one of those 'I'm trying to teach you a lesson' moments?"

"Is it working?" Mom asked.

A gift was sitting on the breakfast table.

"What's this?" asked Samantha.

"It's your new best friend," answered Mom. Samantha unwrapped an alarm clock. A smile crept over her face.

## STORY QUESTIONS

1. What did Samantha's mom mean by saying that the alarm clock would be her best friend?
   a. The alarm would be her only friend.
   b. She knew Samantha needed friends.
   c. She knew that Samantha would learn to rely on the alarm clock.
   d. She was trying to show her that she was being serious.

2. After reading the passage, what is a word that could be used to describe Samantha?
   a. studious
   b. talented
   c. lazy
   d. honest

3. Samantha's mom could be described as . . .
   a. a pushover.
   b. wanting to teach.
   c. unhappy and unsettled.

# THE ATTACK AT MIDNIGHT

Something moved in the cupboard.  It was quite dark this late at night.  In fact, the clock had just chimed midnight.  At the bottom of the cupboard, under a heap of old shoes and clothing not worn for years, was a cardboard box.  Inside the box were some dusty, faded items.  There were old toys, books, and sheets.  Something in the box moved.  Kelsee knew that something had moved because she was carrying the box.  She screamed and dropped it on the floor.

She had worked all day to help her grandmother move into her new house.  Her grandmother was moving closer to Kelsee's family, but this was a difficult move.  She was leaving many memories and items behind.  Grandma Kate had lived in the house for decades.  It had been the family homestead for many years.

Kelsee's dad had managed to convince Grandma to move.  The house was falling into disrepair, and there was no way to keep up with it.  The city had bought the old house and had plans to restore it.

Kelsee ran to get her dad to help her with the box.  There was no way she was going to carry that thing if it had a mouse in it.  Kelsee's dad rummaged through the box but was unable to find anything alive.

"Just one more box," he encouraged.  Kelsee picked up the box and began to carry it upstairs.  Just then something jumped out of the box.

## STORY QUESTIONS

1. What is meant by the term *disrepair* as used in the story?
   a. unorganized
   b. needing to be fixed
   c. historical
   d. easy to repair

2. What do you think Kelsee's response will be to the last incident?
   a. Kelsee will get upset with her father.
   b. Kelsee will carry the box upstairs.
   c. Kelsee will throw the box and scream.
   d. Kelsee will try to catch the thing that jumped from the box.

3. Which sentence from the story will help you predict Kelsee's reaction?
   a. She screamed and dropped it to the floor.
   b. Kelsee ran to get her dad to help her with the box.
   c. She had worked all day to help her grandmother move into her new house.
   d. It had been the family homestead for many years.

# FADED MEMORIES

Jason didn't know where he was. He looked out of the window, but nothing seemed familiar. The room was strange, too. He didn't recognize any of the furniture. Was this his room? He seemed to be fading in and out of consciousness.

And his clothes! They seemed to fit, but he didn't recognize any of them either. He was trying to figure out what was going on when the door opened. He let out a huge sigh of relief when he saw his mother walk into the room.

"Mom! What is going on?" asked Jason.

"Jason. It's so good to see you awake. You've been asleep now for almost an hour."

"What happened?" asked Jason. "Why am I wearing these clothes?"

"Don't you remember what happened? You put on your cousin's cowboy clothes and hopped up on that animal like you were born to ride. It didn't take long before everyone realized that you weren't a real cowboy."

"Oh, man. That must be why my head hurts. Did I hit it when I got bucked off the horse?" asked Jason.

"What horse?" asked Mom. "The only things in that corral were you and a bull."

Jason's eyes got big and round.

## STORY QUESTIONS

1. What does the word *consciousness* mean?
   a. intelligence
   b. awareness
   c. common sense
   d. wakefulness

2. Is Jason proud of his bull-riding experience?
   a. No, he doesn't know what a bull is.
   b. Yes, he is proud that he even got on a bull.
   c. No, he was surprised to find out he had been on a bull.
   d. Yes, he was hoping to have won the competition.

3. Which sentence helps answer the question above?
   a. "Why am I wearing these clothes?"
   b. "Did I hit it when I got bucked off the horse?"
   c. "That must be why my head hurts."
   d. Jason's eyes got big and round.

# MYSTERY SOLVED

Sarah was bored. She didn't have school today, and it was only nine o' clock. Looking through the window, she could see that her friend, Mel, was outside staring at the goldfish swimming around in their pond. Mel was Sarah's next-door neighbor. Just then, the telephone rang. Sarah went to answer the phone, but tripped on a book and fell. "Hello?" she asked tensely, trying to hold back the pain.

"Is that you, Sarah?" asked Mel. "You have to see my goldfish."

"Mel!" Sarah answered sternly. "I tripped getting the phone, and all you are calling for is to see your fish?" Sarah glared through the window at Mel, who smiled up at her.

"You've got to come see this, Sarah. My goldfish have changed color."

Mel was always coming up with crazy ideas and stunts to pull. Sarah put the receiver down and headed downstairs to see Mel. This time she was surprised to see red goldfish swimming around.

"What happened?" asked Sarah.

"I don't know!" replied Mel. "All I know is that last night they were fine."

Just then Sarah noticed some garbage behind the fishpond. She pulled out a wrapper. It was a powdered-drink wrapper.

"Mel! Your fish turned red because you put red drink in their water."

Mel smiled up sheepishly at Sarah and said, "You passed! I didn't think you'd be able to solve this mystery. Come on. Let's go see if there are some other mysteries to solve in the neighborhood."

## STORY QUESTIONS

1. Which of the following statements would be new information to the reader?
   a. Sarah was bored before Mel called.
   b. Sarah doesn't like goldfish.
   c. Mel wants Sarah to try and solve the mystery about his goldfish.
   d. Mel and Sarah are friends.

2. Which sentence explains the problem in this story?
   a. "Let's go see if there are some mysteries to solve in the neighborhood."
   b. Mel was Sarah's next-door neighbor.
   c. Sarah was bored.
   d. Mel's goldfish have changed color.

3. What is the resolution to the story?
   a. It was a powdered-drink wrapper.
   b. "Is that you, Sarah?"
   c. "I tripped getting the phone."
   d. "Let's go see if there are some mysteries to solve in the neighborhood."

Name _____

Date _____

# MY DOG ATE IT

Kendra climbed the steps to her school slowly and methodically. She was sure that she had lost yet another homework assignment. She had done it alright, but she couldn't remember if she had put it in her backpack. It was too late to do anything about it now. The school bus was already gone and the first bell was about to ring.

Kendra was tired of her teacher thinking that she always made mistakes. That wasn't the real Kendra at all. Things were just a little hectic at home. She began thinking of a few excuses she could use.

She wondered if her teacher would believe a story about her homework falling in the bathtub. That just didn't seem very realistic. How about an alien coming from outer space in her dream? Her teacher didn't seem too keen on Kendra's "dream" excuses.

Kendra began dragging her feet as she got to the classroom door. She wished she had a dog so the "dog ate my homework" excuse would work. Kendra's teacher smiled down as Kendra entered the room. How could she let this woman down again?

The teacher had already begun to take roll. Kendra knew that she would ask for homework next. Just then, Kendra heard her name. Before she could answer, her teacher said, "Kendra, I had a nice visit with your mom this morning. She said you forgot your homework, and she dropped it by on her way to work. Wasn't that nice of her?"

## STORY QUESTIONS

1. Which paragraph explains the problem in the story?
   a. first paragraph
   b. last paragraph
   c. third paragraph
   d. fourth paragraph

2. What inferences can you make about the Kendra?
   a. She and her mother don't get along.
   b. She has a hard time getting her homework turned in.
   c. Her teacher assigns strict homework.
   d. Kendra rides her bike to school.

3. What is the meaning of the word *methodically* as used in the story?
   a. firs
   b. quickly
   c. instrumental
   d. systematically

# SKI BUDDIES

It had snowed all night, and the ski runs were filled with powder. It was going to be a great ski day. Max and his friend Greg were trying to hit the runs early. They would meet up with their friend Phillip in the afternoon. Phillip was just learning to ski, and Max and Greg wanted to give him some lessons.

Swoosh! Max flew down the hill with a big smile on his face. He loved to ski. Max saw Greg just ahead of him, and he decided to catch up. He raced down. In fact, he raced down so quickly that his ski got caught on the back of Greg's skis. This sent Max flying head over heels into a snow bank.

Greg skidded to a stop and hollered out, "Max, are you okay?"

Max wasn't sure what to think. His skis were all jumbled, and his poles were somewhere else. His head was throbbing and his arm felt as though it had been bent backwards.

"Yeah, I think I'm alright."

Just then, the ski patrol skied up to see what the trouble was. Max couldn't stand on his ankle. The ski patrol helped Max onto the stretcher and told him they'd take him to First Aid to get checked out.

Max was awfully embarrassed. He was even more embarrassed when he saw Phillip walking by. Phillip's eyes grew wide. Max just knew he had ruined the idea of skiing for Phillip.

He called out, "Phillip, don't worry. This is all just a publicity stunt!"

## STORY QUESTIONS

1. Using inference, what were Phillip's feelings about skiing?
   a. indifferent
   c. worried
   b. disapproves
   d. approves

2. Which sentence indicates Phillip's feelings about skiing?
   a. Phillip's eyes grew wide.
   b. His skis were all jumbled, and his poles were somewhere else.
   c. He was even more embarrassed when he saw Phillip walking by.
   d. "Yeah, I think I'm alright."

3. Which sentence does <u>not</u> refer to Max's feelings about skiing?
   a. Max flew down the hill with a big smile on his face.
   b. He loved to ski.
   c. Max was the best skier in his class.
   d. Max and his friend Greg were trying to hit the runs early.

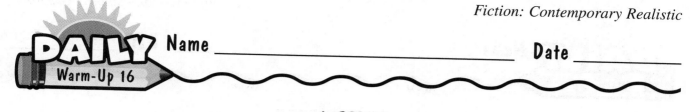

*Fiction: Contemporary Realistic*

# I SPY!

"You were spying on me!" she said, her face red with anger.

"No I wasn't! I didn't know you were here. I was looking for . . ."

"Looking for what?"

"I can't tell you."

"You can't tell me because you weren't looking for anything. You were spying on me!" Harriet stomped her feet as she walked out of the closet. She was sick of her cousin Henry following her, and she was tired of him spying on her. She and her friend Rhonda were trying to have some private time. Henry made that very difficult.

Henry came to spend the summer each year with Harriet's family. Years ago, Harriet enjoyed his company. But these days, just seeing him bothered her. It wasn't that Henry did anything wrong—he just stuck to her like glue.

Harriet and Rhonda packed up their toys and took them somewhere else. Rhonda was familiar with Henry. Harriet had talked about him many times.

Just then, a light bulb went off in Harriet's head. She called after Henry and told him to come back. He did. She made him stay right by her side the rest of the afternoon. Even when he tried to leave, Harriet made him come back. By the end of the first day, Henry was sick of Harriet. Harriet knew that when Henry begged to leave, she had succeeded. For the rest of the week, Henry always found something else to do.

## STORY QUESTIONS

1. Which statement best explains what Harriet did to keep Henry from spying?
   a. Harriet included Henry in what they were playing.
   b. Henry got in trouble each time he left Harriet's side.
   c. Harriet included him so much that he got tired of it.
   d. Harriet refused to let Henry play with them.

2. Which sentence explains the problem in the story?
   a. Harriet was rude to her cousin Henry.
   b. Henry wouldn't leave Harriet alone.
   c. Harriet had talked about him many times.
   d. Henry always found something else to do.

3. Which statement shows whether or not Harriet's plan worked?
   a. He stuck to her like glue.
   b. Harriet enjoyed his company.
   c. Harriet made him come back.
   d. Henry always found something else to do.

4. What is the meaning of the word *private* in the story?
   a. unbiased and disinterested
   b. secretive and confidential
   c. you can't tell from reading the passage
   d. on their own

# THE CAVE

Jacob crawled on his stomach through the passageway in the cave. He was very anxious to see light at the end. It had been a long day. He was cold, hungry, and exhausted. As he crept along, questions were flooding through his mind. Would he ever see his family again? Was he going to make it out alive? He was sure that he could make it if he could just find light.

Just then, the noise at the back of the cave started again. The noise was louder than it ever was before. Jacob still couldn't decide what it was, but he wasn't about to wait and find out.

Jacob kept his head tucked low. He knew that if what made the noise could fly, he didn't want to get hit. Just then Jacob's hand hit against something rough. He spread his fingers wide and wiped them over the object. It was his flashlight! With excitement, he quickly and quietly turned it on. Jacob strained his eyes to look in the direction of the noise.

There was a large box dangling from the cave by a rope. Every time the box hit the side of the cave, it made a large noise. That was the noise Jacob had heard. But why was the box swaying? It finally occurred to Jacob that there was a slight breeze. If he followed the direction of the breeze, he could find his way out! With a smile on his face, Jacob worked his way to the entrance of the cave.

## STORY QUESTIONS

1. Which word best describes how Jacob felt at the end of the story?
   a. organized
   b. relieved
   c. annoyed
   d. exhausted

2. Which paragraph helps you answer the previous question?
   a. second paragraph
   b. first paragraph
   c. fourth paragraph
   d. third paragraph

3. Another title for this passage could be . . .
   a. "Jacob's Day in the Cave."
   b. "Jacob's New Adventure."
   c. "Jacob Attacks the Noise."
   d. "Jacob Discovers the Noise."

# IRONING BOARD SURFING

Charles had been looking forward to his summer vacation with his family. He was excited to go to the beach. His parents finally agreed to let his best friend Henry come along. Henry and Charles had been practicing their surfing on his mom's ironing board.

Despite the broken hinges and the goose egg on Henry's head, practicing had gone well. The six-hour drive to the beach passed quickly, as Charles and Henry had video game competitions.

They finally arrived at the beach and set up camp that night. Henry and Charles could hardly sleep. As the sun was peeking over the hills, the boys were trotting down the beach to catch some waves. As they paddled through the water and turned to catch a wave, they quickly learned that their ironing-board training was inadequate for the strength of the ocean.

In their focus and concentration, the boys lost track of time. They decided to head in for lunch. Fighting the waves, they finally made it to shore. As they walked across the sand, they found themselves on strange beach they did not recognize. Charles' parents were nowhere in sight. There wasn't a single person on the beach.

"Whoa!" exclaimed Henry.

"What are we going to do?" moaned Charles.

## STORY QUESTIONS

*1.* According to the story, Henry and Charles are . . .
   a. intelligent.
   b. immature.
   c. friends.
   d. only children.

*2.* Which paragraph helps you answer the previous question?
   a. second paragraph
   b. first paragraph
   c. fourth paragraph
   d. third paragraph

*3.* Why was the ironing board not good for training?
   a. It is heavier than a surf board.
   b. It is not the right shape of the surf board.
   c. The waves were too strong.
   d. The ironing board was broken.

# APRIL FOOL'S DAY

Adam's frustration started as soon as he opened his eyes. He woke up to the fire alarm blaring in his ear. Adam never really believed in April Fool's Day, but on this particular day, he was beginning to wonder. When he went to brush his teeth, his toothbrush was nowhere to be found. It took him 20 minutes to find his jacket—which happened to be in the garage, of all places. How on Earth did it get there?

Adam was late for school because his mother couldn't find her car keys. When it came time to turn in his homework, Adam was not surprised to see that it wasn't in his backpack, even though he vividly remembered putting it in the backpack that morning. What was he going to do? What was going on?

Adam shuffled his feet as he walked to the office to get an I.O.U. He had lost his lunch ticket somewhere between the classroom and the cafeteria. He was about to give, up when he saw his friend Fred walking down the hallway towards him. Fred had the biggest smile on his face. As Fred passed, he laughed out loud. Adam wondered what it was all about.

"Fred, what's going on?" asked Adam.

"You really don't get this, do you?" questioned Fred.

"Do you really think that the spell you put on me yesterday really worked?" Adam asked incredulously. Fred continued chuckling as he walked down the hall.

## STORY QUESTIONS

1. What do the initials *I.O.U.* stand for?
   a. I order you
   b. I open your door
   c. I owe you
   d. I own you

2. Adam doesn't believe Fred's spell worked because . . .
   a. he doesn't believe in things like that.
   b. the spell wasn't strong enough.
   c. he knows that Fred is just teasing.
   d. Fred is not experienced enough to cast spells.

3. What is another possible title for this story passage?
   a. "Adam's Day of Awakening"      c. "Adam Learns his Lesson"
   b. "Fred's Frustrating Spell"        d. "Anger Management"

# THE TREASURE

It was a hot, sunny day in June when Miranda and Jessica, who had recently become friends, were exploring in the vacant lot at the end of the street. Miranda had lived her whole life in this neighborhood, but Jessica had moved in just two months ago. The vacant lot was filled with wild flowers, weeds, and litter. Miranda and Jessica were hoping to find something exciting to cure their boredom.

"Hey! Look at this!" called Miranda.

"What is it?" asked Jessica.

"It looks like a message."

Jessica hurried to catch up with Miranda. Miranda was peering over a tattered piece of paper. Her eyes got bigger and bigger as she read.

"What does it say?" asked Jessica.

"It says that a treasure was buried here! I just can't believe it!" exclaimed Miranda. The girls screamed excitedly and began to follow the directions written in the letter. The first clue sent them to the back of the lot. From there, they found another clue that sent them to the garbage cans. Under the biggest garbage can was another note. Miranda and Jessica just couldn't believe it. Things were falling into place too easily.

They were right. In the midst of reading another clue, Jason jumped out from behind the garbage can laughing. The girls were mad! They took off screaming and tried to catch Jason.

## STORY QUESTIONS

1. According to the story, Miranda and Jessica are . . .
   a. bored and frustrated.
   b. unsure about the treasure hunt.
   c. enjoying the treasure hunt.
   d. going shopping when they get home.

2. Which paragraph explains how long Miranda and Jessica have been friends?
   a. second paragraph          c. fourth paragraph
   b. first paragraph           d. third paragraph

3. At the end of the passage, Miranda and Jessica realize they have been . . .
   a. honest.
   b. tricked.
   c. amazed.
   d. busy.

**DAILY Warm-Up 5**

Name _____ Date _____

# THE CHESS CHAMPION

Geoffrey looked down at the chessboard and swallowed. He could feel sweat starting to form on his forehead. He glanced at this competitor across the table. The boy was staring at the chessboard with a smile on his face.

"Is it over?" thought Geoffrey, "or can I pull this off?"

Geoffrey shifted weight from his left foot to his right foot. He nervously moved one of his pawns. The game was reaching a climax. Geoffrey struggled to figure out what his competitor was thinking. If he could figure out his strategy, he could prevent any damage.

His competitor quickly moved one of his pawns as well. Geoffrey looked up at his competitor again. He could see a drop of sweat. Could it be? Geoffrey soon realized that his competitor was just as nervous as he was.

Geoffrey gained confidence and quickly moved his knight on his next move. After studying the board, he soon realized he could end the game with three more moves. Geoffrey smiled and wiped his brow dry.

Just then, Geoffrey's competitor called out, "Checkmate!" Geoffrey looked down at the board in disbelief.

## STORY QUESTIONS

1. Which word best describes how Geoffrey was feeling at the beginning of the passage?
   a. nervous
   b. happy
   c. relieved
   d. overwhelmed

2. Which statement from the passage describes how Geoffrey was feeling at the beginning of the passage?
   a. He glanced at this competitor across the table.
   b. Geoffrey looked down at the chessboard and swallowed.
   c. He could see a drop of sweat.
   d. The boy was staring at the chessboard with a smile on his face.

3. Why did Geoffrey look up at his competitor again?
   a. He was scared of his competitor.
   b. He was trying to cheat.
   c. He was planning his next move.
   d. He was trying to see how his competitor was feeling.

# HERE COMES THE DOG!

Alex was so excited to ride his new bike to school in the morning. He had just received the bike for his birthday, but he had never ridden it to school. Alex's friend, Bo, promised to meet him on the corner so that they could ride together.

Alex got ready for bed. He could hardly sleep. He wondered why he felt so nervous. He had walked this path hundreds of times, but riding a bike was different. There was a section of busy traffic that was a bit dangerous.

The next morning, Alex was up bright and early. He gulped down his oatmeal at breakfast and kissed his mom goodbye before she had a chance to ask any questions. He snapped on his bike helmet and pulled the bike out of the garage.

Off in the distance, Alex could see Bo. Alex took a deep breath and hopped on. As Bo rode past, Alex pushed his pedals to catch up. It was going to be a great day.

Just then, a blur raced right out in front of Alex. He froze and slammed on the brakes. Before Alex could stop, he hit the blur, sailed through the air, and landed on the hard cement. Alex groaned as he tried to raise his arm. He knew it was probably broken. What was that? Was it a speed bump? Just then, Mrs. Kroeger's little dog began licking Alex's face. Alex smiled when he realized what the blur really was.

## STORY QUESTIONS

1. What is the problem in this story?
   a. Alex doesn't know how to ride the bike.
   b. Alex is an amateur.
   c. Alex hits a dog on his bike.
   d. Alex is chasing dogs on his bike.

2. After reading the passage, which of the following statements do you think would be something Alex would say?
   a. "I've got to beat Bo to school today."
   b. "I hope I can make it to school today without any problems on the bike."
   c. "I can't wait to hit Mrs. Kroeger's dog."
   d. "I need a new bike!"

3. Why did Alex smile when he realized what he had hit?
   a. Alex was happy when he finally hit the dog.
   b. He knew Mrs. Kroeger would be upset if he didn't pet the dog.
   c. The dog's licking made him smile, and he was relieved the dog wasn't hurt.
   d. He knew Bo was watching him.

# THE PEEPING TOM

Samantha was excited to have all of her friends coming over for a slumber party after school that day. She had been waiting all week for the big day. Just as the last bell rang at school, Samantha hopped on her bike and pedaled home.

Samantha's mom greeted her at the door. Her mom had decorated the kitchen with balloons and crepe paper. This was going to be an awesome party. Before long, the pizza was delivered and the girls were beginning to show up.

After dinner, the girls went downstairs to watch a video. The video was in full swing when Samantha noticed something unusual going on outside. She slowly crawled to the window and peered outside.

"What are you doing, Sam?" asked Amy.

"Just looking," replied Samantha. "It looks like there is a person in the vacant house next door."

"Stop it! You are freaking me out!" commented Aubrey. She was always afraid of everything.

"I'm being serious!" said Samantha. She opened the curtains wide for all the girls to see. The girls were stunned to see a pair of eyes staring back at them from next door.

"Ahhhh!" they all screamed, and they went running upstairs.

"Mom! There is a creepy man next door! He's staring at us!" yelled Samantha.

"Oh. That must be our new neighbor, Mr. Jones," answered Mom calmly. "He just moved in today." Samantha's breathing slowly calmed down. She was going to have to think of something neighborly that she could do to make up for her rudeness. But for now, she was content to finish her movie and eat some more popcorn.

## STORY QUESTIONS

1. What does the term "freaking me out" mean in this story?
   a. You are annoying me.
   b. You are acting smarter than me.
   c. You are making me sick.
   d. You are scaring me.

2. Which sentence resolves the problem in the story?
   a. Samantha's breathing slowly calmed down.
   b. "Oh. That must be our new neighbor, Mr. Jones," answered Mom calmly. "He just moved in today."
   c. "There is a creepy man next door!"

3. Which is another good title for this story passage?
   a. "Samantha's New Neighbor"
   b. "Scary Sleepover Trick"
   c. "Samantha Goes Crazy"

# THE MISSING SHOE

Girl Scout Troop #401 was hiking down the trail towards the cabin. They had been hiking for over an hour. All the girls on the trip were experienced campers. Though they had taken the hike many times, they never tired of maneuvering through the rocky terrain.

Jennifer climbed over the last big hurdle in the climb when she stopped short and stared at the trail ahead of her. Becky bumped into Jennifer's back.

"What are you doing?" asked Becky.

"Looking at this shoe. What is it doing on the trail?" replied Jennifer. "I've never seen a shoe in the trail before. Why would someone take their shoe off and leave it here?"

"That is awfully strange," said Mrs. Jones, their Girl Scout leader. "Let's just leave it here."

The girls continued their hike, but it wasn't long before they noticed a shirt on the trail. They all agreed that this was weird! As the girls continued walking, they noticed a tent off to the side, but no one was around. Not too far from the tent was another shoe.

"Do you think someone needs help?" asked Jennifer.

"They do need help. They need help from that big fluffy dog!" laughed Mrs. Jones.

A little further down the trail was a white dog with a shirt in its mouth. The dog had been spreading clothes all over the place. The girls chuckled as they finished their hike.

## STORY QUESTIONS

1. Who is the main character in this story?
   a. Mrs. Jones
   b. Becky
   c. Jennifer

2. What do you think will probably happen next in the story?
   a. The camper who owns the dog will see what the dog did.
   b. The dog will begin to spread the girls' clothes around.
   c. The dog will get sick from eating clothes.
   d. The dog will be picked up by a camper and taken to lost and found.

3. Where is the setting of the story?
   a. in the cabin
   b. in the Girl Scout troop
   c. on a rock
   d. on the trail

Name _____ Date _____

## THE MYSTERIOUS MAIL

Each day, Clara checked the mail for a letter from her Aunt Jill. Aunt Jill was her favorite aunt, and each summer she got to spend a week with her in Colorado. Clara knew it was time for the letter to arrive listing the details of her pending trip, but there was nothing from Aunt Jill in the mailbox today.

But there was something: a letter with Clara's name on it—her first name only. It was written in creepy handwriting. It was the third letter like it to come in three days, but Clara was too afraid to open the letters. Clara was starting to get worried. She brought the mail into the house and hollered upstairs to her mom that the mail was in.

"Did I get anything?" called her mother.

"No, but I did," answered Clara.

"Is it another one of those weird letters?" asked Mom.

"It is, and I'm getting sick of it. This is getting scary," stated Clara.

There was a letter like that in the mailbox for the next two days. Clara was getting scared. Was it from a stalker? Clara couldn't imagine who it could be.

The next morning Clara got a phone call from her Aunt Jill. She was so excited.

"Hi, Clara," said Aunt Jill. "Have you been getting my letters?"

"That's just it, Aunt Jill," said Clara, "You haven't sent any!"

"I've sent you one every day for the past week!" stated Aunt Jill.

Just then the light bulb went off in Clara's head and she began laughing and laughing.

## STORY QUESTIONS

1. According to the story, Jill and Clara are . . .
   a. friends.
   b. interesting.
   c. related.
   d. children.

2. Which sentence from the story would help you answer the previous question?
   a. A letter with Clara's name on it.
   b. It was written in creepy handwriting.
   c. It was the third letter in three days.
   d. Clara checked the mail for a letter from her Aunt Jill.

3. Why did Clara not realize the letters were from her Aunt Jill?
   a. They came differently than before, with only her first name on them.
   b. She was not expecting a letter from her Aunt Jill.
   c. She knew her Aunt Jill wouldn't send her so many letters.
   d. Her summer trip was canceled, so there was no need to receive any.

**DAILY** Warm-Up 10

Name _____

Date _____

# THE STOLEN BIKE

Chris ran to the door of the school building. He couldn't wait to get home. He knew his trading cards would be in the mailbox waiting for him. He came to a screeching halt at the bike rack and scanned the bikes looking for his bike.

"What?" cried Chris. He couldn't see his bike anywhere. He searched and searched again, but he couldn't find his bike. Anger raged through his body as he made his way to the principal's office. He couldn't believe someone had the nerve to steal his bike.

After he reported the crime, he hurried home. Chris tore the package open and began sifting through the cards. Just then, his friend called to see if he could meet him at the park for baseball. Chris set out on foot towards the park. "Oh! This makes me so mad! I wish I had my bike."

The next morning Chris got a ride to school. After school, he walked home. It was a hot walk home without the bike.

"They found your bike," his mother stated calmly.

"What? Where?" asked Chris.

"It's in the garage where you left it," said Mom.

"No way!" said Chris.

He threw open the garage door, only to find his bike gleaming up at him. Chris was thrilled and embarrassed. That night over dinner, he shared the story and a laugh with his family.

## STORY QUESTIONS

1. How did Chris feel about finding his bike in the garage?
   a. embarrassed
   b. angry
   c. frustrated
   d. expectant

2. Which paragraph helps you answer the previous question?
   a. second paragraph
   b. first paragraph
   c. fourth paragraph
   d. last paragraph

3. Which of the following quotes was from Chris?
   a. "Of course!"
   b. "They found your bike."
   c. "Oh, it's in the garage where you left it."
   d. "No way!"

# WILD THINGS IN THE CLOSET

Brenda ran in the door. She was running late, as usual. She raced up the stairs and grabbed her clothes. She jumped in the shower as fast as she could. Out of the corner of her eye, she thought she saw a snake.

But how could that be? It was the dead of winter. Snakes wouldn't be lurking around now. Besides, what would a snake be doing in the house? Brenda wiped her wet hair with a towel. She wanted to get it as dry as she could before she had to go.

Brenda's mom called from downstairs. It was time to go. Brenda grabbed her tennis shoes and her purse. As she looked down at her hands, she let out a blood-curdling scream. It wasn't the handle of her purse—it was a snake, a real live snake!

It didn't take long for Brenda's brother to capture the reptile and take it outside. Brenda told herself to trust her instincts from now on. She had been right! The snake obviously didn't know what time of year it was, and it certainly didn't know whose room it had tried to invade.

## STORY QUESTIONS

1. Which statement shows the climax of the story?
   a. As she looked down at her hands, she let out a blood-curdling scream.
   b. It didn't take long for Brenda's brother to capture the reptile and take it outside.
   c. Brenda's mom called from downstairs.
   d. She wanted to get it as dry as she could before she had to go.

2. What does the word *lurking* mean?
   a. projecting
   b. opening up
   c. observing
   d. creeping around

3. What is the main idea of the third paragraph?
   a. Brenda is trying to get her brother to come get the snake.
   b. Brenda is trying to dry her hair as fast as she can.
   c. Brenda is shocked that a real snake is in her room.

4. Which paragraph shows the resolution of the story?
   a. first paragraph
   b. second paragraph
   c. third paragraph
   d. none of the above

# THE SECRET FRIEND

Someone knew Allison's name. She couldn't believe it. Here she was at her new school for less than an hour, and someone was calling her name. There must be some mistake! Allison slammed her locker shut and ducked into the crowd. She wanted to see who was calling her. It was hard enough to be the new kid, but to have a stalker, too!

A few feet away, Allison stepped behind a locker. A tall, thin girl with curly hair was calling her name. Allison didn't have a clue who she was. She slipped into class. She had to think about this.

After class, Allison stepped into the hallway again. She couldn't believe it when she heard her name again. She slipped into another classroom and watched as the girl walked by. Who was she? Allison had some detective work to do.

At lunch, Allison was eating alone. She was thinking about her friends back home and began feeling lonely.

The tall, thin girl walked up to her table. "Hi. I'm Angie," the girl said. "I'm your secret pal. I've been trying to catch up with you all day! I wanted to make sure you had at least one friend today."

Allison couldn't believe it. She had been dodging her new best friend all morning. "Wow. Thanks," said Allison. "Why don't you call me Ally, like my friends do?" Suddenly, Ally didn't feel so lonely anymore. Instead, a sheepish smile crossed her face as she thought about how silly she had been.

## STORY QUESTIONS

1. Which words describe Allison in the story?
   a. new, outgoing, confident
   b. timid, shy, new
   c. timid, obnoxious, scared
   d. stuck up, timid, excited

2. Which of the following statements is <u>not</u> accurate?
   a. Angie was calling Allison's name all morning.
   b. Angie was trying to meet her secret pal.
   c. Angie was lost and needed help from Allison.
   d. Allison was worried someone was stalking her.

3. What is the problem in the story?
   a. Allison is feeling sorry for herself.
   b. Allison felt like someone was following her at her new school.
   c. Allison was new at school.
   d. Allison was nervous about meeting new people.

**Name** _____   **Date** _____

## S.O.S.

Jake jumped into the ocean for one last swim of the season. It had been a wonderful summer. He had no regrets. His surfing skills had dramatically improved. The feel of the ocean water on his skin was heavenly. Jake kicked his flippers and pushed deeper into the water.

Just then, Jake felt a stinging sensation going down his leg. He glanced down, but the water was too murky to see much. Jake froze in the water. He didn't know what to do. If he moved, he might get hurt even worse. Was it a shark? A biting fish? Fear settled into Jake's body and he remained as motionless as he could. What was he going to do?

The pain was getting worse so Jake decided to move. He lunged forward but felt another stinging sensation on his belly. He realized that he had to move—and fast! The pain was severe, and he was beginning to feel weak. He glanced up and saw his friend David swimming nearby. He called for David to come and help him. It didn't take long before David was right alongside him assessing the situation. David cradled Jake and helped him to shore.

The parents all gathered around to offer first aid and help. Jake would be okay. He had been stung by a stingray. In the commotion, he saw David through the crowd and smiled at him. Jake had just seen a true friend in action, and he knew it!

## STORY QUESTIONS

1. What was Jake's dilemma?
   a. deciding whether to move or stay put in the water
   b. deciding whether to go swimming that day or not
   c. deciding whether to trust David or not
   d. deciding whether to swim deeper or not

2. What would make another good title for this story?
   a. "The Exciting Situation"
   b. "David vs. the Stingray"
   c. "A Call for Help"
   d. "David and Jake"

3. What does the word *murky* mean?
   a. piloted
   b. freshwater
   c. depressed
   d. dark and cloudy

# PUPPY LOVE

It wasn't the prettiest dog around, but it was a puppy. No matter the breed, a puppy is always cute. Gretchen had wanted a dog for as long as she could remember, but her parents had always said no. This time was different. The puppy had been hanging around their house for two days. It whimpered and seemed hungry. On the second night, Gretchen fed it some of her hot dog. It hadn't left her side since.

The next morning, Gretchen's parents called the pound and reported the missing puppy. They were told that if no one claimed the puppy in 72 hours, the puppy could be theirs. They didn't seem too worried. They knew the owner would show up.

Two days went by without a call. On the third day, it happened. Everyone froze. Gretchen's father answered the phone. Whew! It wasn't the pound. Thirty minutes later, the phone rang again. Gretchen gasped for air. It was someone selling soaps. Late in the evening, the phone rang again. This time it was the pound.

The owner showed up at Gretchen's house the next morning. Gretchen hadn't slept at all that night. She couldn't believe it was over. But the owner asked if the family would be interested in adopting the puppy. Gretchen couldn't believe her ears. This was the last pup in the litter. They had been trying to find an owner. The smile on her parents' faces made Gretchen realize that she was the proud owner of little Miracle.

## STORY QUESTIONS

1. What is this passage mainly about?
   a. how a puppy can get lost
   b. the process an owner takes to find a lost animal
   c. the different types of dogs
   d. how Gretchen finally received a dog

2. In the third paragraph, what does the word *gasped* mean?
   a. quickly took in air
   b. documented
   c. measured
   d. opened

3. What improved Gretchen's chances of finally getting a dog?
   a. A puppy is hard to house train.
   b. An adorable puppy is hard to refuse.
   c. An adorable puppy is hard to sell.
   d. Her parents decided a dog isn't so bad.

4. Why did Gretchen name her puppy Miracle?
   a. It was a miracle the puppy had not died.
   b. Her parents believe in miracles.
   c. It was a miracle that Gretchen's parents let her keep the dog.
   d. She had always wanted to name a dog Miracle.

# ALARMING DISCOVERY

The alarm went off at 5:00 A.M like it did every morning. Megan rolled over and tried to open her eyes. Was it morning already? She practically fell off the bed and threw her legs in her jeans. It was a cold morning. She buttoned up her winter coat and headed outside.

Megan fed her cow each morning this early so that she could catch the school bus into town. Last summer, Megan's father had given her a cow of her very own. The cow had not been feeling well, so Megan was feeding it hay.

Megan grabbed a bale of hay and hauled it over to the pen. Daisy the cow was going to be happy this morning. The sun was far from up, yet she was already getting her breakfast. Megan tossed the bale of hay up to the fence post and leaned over to gently drop it down.

Megan was just about to get the next bale when she stopped dead in her tracks. The pen was empty, and the fence was broken. In a panic Megan searched the barn, calling Daisy's name. She was nowhere to be found. Megan's search continued for another 20 minutes.

Just past the cottonwood tree, Megan heard a noise. She turned back to get a second look. To her amazement, there on the ground sat Daisy . . . and her new baby calf. Megan just sat on the ground and laughed. This was going to be a crazy day!

## STORY QUESTIONS

1. Why was Megan so surprised when she found Daisy?
   a. Daisy had been lost for over an hour.
   b. She was worried that Daisy had died.
   c. She was surprised to discover that Daisy had a baby calf.
   d. She was surprised that Daisy wasn't in her pen.

2. What can you learn about Megan from reading this passage?
   a. She lives in a city.
   b. She loves to read about cows.
   c. She was born blind.
   d. She is a hard worker.

3. Which of the following statements is accurate?
   a. Daisy was getting out of her pen on a daily basis.
   b. Megan was tired of caring for her cow, Daisy.
   c. Megan's father was upset with how Megan was caring for Daisy.
   d. none of the above

**DAILY** Warm-Up 16

Name _____

Date _____

# RACING FOR FRIENDSHIP

Jeff and Kirk were racing down the hill on their mountain bikes. They'd been on the trail numerous times before. They took turns winning the race. Kyle and Greg were at the base of the hill waiting to see who would make it first this time.

At the curve of the hill, a deer was waiting by the side of the road. It heard the noise from the boys. It was trying to decide whether or not it should find another place to hide.

As Jeff and Kirk were speeding down, Kirk let out a whoop and a holler. It was just enough to scare the deer, and it leaped onto the road—right in front of the racing boys. Was it all over? This was going to be bad.

The look on Jeff's face showed that this was not going to be good. In a split second, Jeff veered sharply to the right, just missing the deer and skidding to a stop. This left just enough room for Kirk to race on down the mountain.

He couldn't stop for quite a while. In fact, when he crossed the imaginary finish line, Kyle and Greg were there to cheer him on.

"You're the winner," they cried! "You did it!"

Kirk was panting and trying to catch his breath. When he finally got his words out he said, "No boys. The winner is still up there on that mountain. When he gets down, let's give him a big cheer."

## STORY QUESTIONS

1. Kirk's definition of friendship includes . . .
   a. similar interests.
   b. sacrifice and courage.
   c. a few arguments.
   d. racing together.

2. According to the passage, how did Jeff save Kirk from a terrible wreck?
   a. He stayed hidden until the right time.
   b. He turned in time and almost wrecked himself.
   c. He let Kirk pass him by.
   d. He ran into the deer in the road.

3. The best way to find the answer to the previous question is to . . .
   a. reread the entire passage.
   b. reread the first paragraph and determine the main idea.
   c. reread the fourth paragraph.
   d. skim the passage and look for clues.

Name _____     Date _____

# THE DISAPPEARING CAT

She just couldn't believe it. Heather had lost her cat. She was devastated. Heather called for her cat over and over, but there was no response. "Chuckles. Oh, Chuckles. Where are you?" Heather wondered if her cat had been stolen. It wasn't like Chuckles to stay away so long.

Chuckles wasn't like any other cat. She was a special cat. She could laugh. Well, at least she could laugh for Heather. Heather would take Chuckles up to her room and they would laugh for hours and hours. Heather had never been able to get Chuckles to laugh with anyone else. It was a special secret the two of them shared.

That night, Heather was watching a television show and laughing at all the jokes. She thought she heard someone else laughing, but when she turned the television down, she didn't hear anything. Later in the show she heard some more laughing. This time she knew it wasn't her imagination. She looked under her bed and under the dresser. No Chuckles. Just then, she got an idea. She went to the window and pressed her ear against the glass. Sure enough, she could hear someone or something laughing. She opened the window, and there sat Chuckles, giggling away at the jokes.

"Get in here, Chuckles," she said, "I sure have missed you."

Chuckles just grinned.

## STORY QUESTIONS

1. Chuckles and Heather shared a . . .
   a. secret.
   b. favorite treat.
   c. funny joke.
   d. bed.

2. According to the passage, how did Heather find Chuckles?
   a. She didn't find Chuckles, her mother did.
   b. She set out some food for Chuckles.
   c. She listened for the sound of laughter.
   d. She told a bunch of jokes.

3. A good way to find the answer to the previous question is to . . .
   a. reread the entire passage.
   b. skim the passage and determine the main idea
   c. reread the third paragraph and search for clues.

4. How did Chuckles get her name?
   a. because of her special talent
   b. because it was an easy name to say
   c. because it was the name of the cat at the pet store
   d. because the cat had learned to talk

Name _____ Date _____

# WILL POWER

One Sunday, I was flipping through the ads with my mom. "Boring, boring," I said. I flipped through the colorful pages. I got to the recreation pages. Then, I saw it! A trampoline! Wow! Then a rush of disappointment filled my body. It wouldn't fit in our backyard.

Just to make sure, I went out in our backyard to check. It is REALLY long, but not very wide. It's like a long creek, without any room. I then decided to measure the backyard. Thirteen feet! Yes! There was just one problem. Would our parents let us get it?

I rushed into the house. "Mama, Mama!" I yelled.

"What?" she asked.

"I measured the backyard and the trampoline will fit!" I shouted.

"Let's go measure it," she said. She went outside with me and I helped her measure the yard. Then my dad came out and my siblings begged them to get it. They replied that there just wouldn't be room.

Later, my mom and dad had a "secret talk" about getting it. Before I knew what was happening, my mom was snapping her fingers and the yard was widening. That's right, the yard began to grow.

The next day after school, when we got home, there was the trampoline waiting for us. It sure is nice to have a mom who has special powers.

## STORY QUESTIONS

*1.* A theme to this story could be . . .
   a. "Dreams granted."
   b. "Make a wish and it will come true."
   c. "If there's a will, there's a way."
   d. "Mom and Dad are the best."

*2.* According to the passage, how did the mother make room for the trampoline?
   a. She snapped her fingers.
   b. She made plans to move.
   c. She cut out a new section for the yard.
   d. She rented a bulldozer.

*3.* A good way to find the answer to question #2 above is to . . .
   a. try to remember.
   b. reread the first paragraph and determine the main idea.
   c. ask the author.
   d. skim the passage searching for clues about the mother.

Name _____ Date _____

# VOLLEYBALL VENUE

Laura and Melissa were good at volleyball. They had played together on the same team for years. Their next game was at 6:00 that night. They had gone to Laura's house to take a break and get a bite to eat.

They raided the refrigerator for something to eat. There wasn't much to be found—that is, except for some round, wet balls. They were clear, soggy things about the size of a tennis ball.

"What on Earth?" asked Laura.

"Oh, yuck! That looks disgusting!" chimed Melissa.

"That's because it is disgusting!" replied Laura.

"Don't you go messing with my monster eyes," called Laura's dad from the other room.

"Monster eyes?" asked Melissa.

"He's being serious," said Laura. "They think they've found the giant monster of the sea they've been looking for all these years. It really exists!"

"Right!" answered Melissa.

At that moment, the house began to shake and pictures began to fall from the wall.

## STORY QUESTIONS

1. Which word best describes Melissa in the story?
   a. confused
   b. annoyed
   c. furious
   d. coy

2. Which of the following statements is <u>not</u> accurate?
   a. Laura's dad says some strange things.
   b. Melissa and Laura are on the same team.
   c. The house begins shaking and moving.
   d. There is a resolution to this story.

3. What is the problem in the story?
   a. Laura is feeling sorry for herself.
   b. Melissa felt like something strange had happened at volleyball.
   c. Something strange is happening at Laura's house.
   d. Melissa was nervous about meeting new people

# MARTIAN MADNESS

The Martian was in every one of Jordan's classes. He was always sitting in Jordan's seat and using Jordan's pencil. Jordan was starting to wonder if he had gone crazy.

The Martian knew his name, but he didn't seem to like Jordan. In first period, he almost got into a fistfight over the chair. Jordan finally gave in, but the Martian insisted that he and Jordan share the chair. And so Jordan shared the chair with the Martian for the rest of the hour. It was the most uncomfortable hour Jordan had ever experienced.

It seemed that Jordan was the only one who could see the Martian, as everyone, including his teachers, gave him funny looks when he tried to talk to the Martian. He had to figure out what the Martian wanted. At lunchtime, the Martian used his lunch ticket and ate his chicken strips. Jordan got strange looks when he would occasionally start talking aloud to the alien.

"So what do you want? Is it my chair? my teachers? my life? Why me?

"No," was the Martian's response. "Your brain."

"My brain?" asked Jordan. "Now that's a funny one. I've been accused on many occasions of not having one!"

## STORY QUESTIONS

*1.* According to the story, the Martian keeps . . .
   a. sleeping in Jordan's bed.
   b. sitting in Jordan's chair.
   c. wearing Jordan's clothes.
   d. waking up Jordan.

*2.* Which sentence from the story helps you answer the previous question?
   a. The Martian knew his name.
   b. "I've been accused on many occasions of not having one!"
   c. In first period, he almost got into a fistfight over the chair.
   d. Jordan got strange looks when he would occasionally start talking aloud to the alien.

*3.* What surprised Jordan about what the Martian wanted?
   a. Jordan was afraid of the Martian.
   b. He couldn't imagine there would be enough to go around.
   c. Jordan would be accused of stealing if he gave it to the Martian.
   d. He wanted something Jordan said others didn't think he had.

DAILY
Warm-Up 5

Name _____    Date _____

# THE QUEST

"Now remember," said Joshua's mother, "I want you home at 2:30—no later than that. Understand?"

"Yes, yes, Mother, I understand," Joshua said angelically. He wasn't a big fan of school, especially these days, since they were studying Egypt. He slowly walked up the steps to his classroom.

"Oh, great!" said his friend Evan sarcastically. "We get to go hear Mr. Jones drone on and on about Egypt!"

A group of boys laughed and started to walk inside the classroom.

"All right, students, let's begin the day with Egypt, shall we?" Mr. Jones called out. Almost all the students groaned inwardly. The class began reading out of their books. Before long, Joshua started to fall asleep. He kept drifting in and out until finally he was asleep.

Joshua felt something warm underneath his feet. It felt like sand. He opened his eyes to find that it was sand. He stood up and found that he was standing next to a pyramid.

"What?" He didn't know where he was. Then he said under his breath, "I'm in Egypt, 2,000 years ago!"

Suddenly, someone yelled, "Hey, you get out of there right now, you tomb-robber! Stay right there, you ruffian!"

Joshua turned to run. He ran into the pyramid and glanced around. It was amazing. He decided that when he got back to Mr. Jones' class, he better pay more attention.

Just then, a group of men came running at Joshua with their knives in the air…

## STORY QUESTIONS

1. Who is the main character in this story?
   a. Mr. Jones          b. Mother          c. Joshua

2. What do you think will most likely happen next in the story?
   a. Joshua will attack the men.
   b. Joshua will hide from the men.
   c. Joshua will ask the men for more information about Egypt.
   d. Joshua will apologize to the men for stealing.

3. What is the main problem in the story?
   a. Mr. Jones is upset with Joshua for          c. Joshua finds himself in a foreign time
      falling asleep in class.                         and place.
   b. Joshua is upset with his mom for            d. none of the above
      scolding him.

Name _____

Date _____

# FOOTBALL PRACTICE

Matthew and John were walking home together after football practice. It was drizzling. It had been a tough practice, but a good one.

"Man, I'm wiped out," said Matthew.

"Me, too," responded John. "I didn't think I was going to make it."

The boys took a shortcut through Mr. Hepner's back yard. They were close to the end of the fence when a bright light beamed down directly overhead.

"Whoa!" hollered Matthew.

"What is that?" wondered John.

Just then, a creature walked through the gate and said, "Hello. I'm here to tell you that you have been chosen."

"Chosen?" asked John.

"Yes," replied the creature.

John took off in a sprint trying to get away. He didn't want to see what happened next. He flipped his agile body over the fence. He was running as fast as he could when he tripped and fell flat on his face. He groaned.

Just then, he heard someone calling his name. Was it the creature? He opened his eyes and saw his coach standing above him. "John, are you okay?"

"Yeah, Coach!" said John. "I just tripped."

"No, you've been lying here for a while. You really got hit on that last tackle. By the way, did you hear you've been chosen to play varsity?"

John smiled. He had been chosen! He jumped up and hurried back to the football field.

## STORY QUESTIONS

1. Did John really see a creature?
   a. Yes. The creature brought him back to the playing field.
   b. Yes. The creature got Matthew instead.
   c. No. John was knocked out and dreaming of the creature.
   d. No. John and Matthew were making up the creature.

2. What is the meaning of the word *agile* as used in the story?
   a. hyper
   b. nimble
   c. chubby
   d. lanky

3. Which character in this story indicates that it is a fantasy story?
   a. Mr. Hepner
   b. the creature
   c. Coach
   d. Matthew

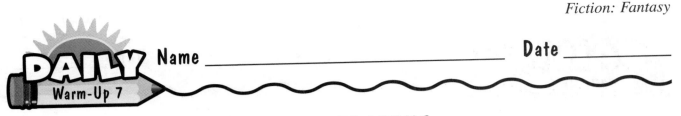

# COMPUTER VIRUS

Landon started up his computer before school like he did every day. His computer was programmed to do his homework. Yes, his computer was like his best friend. Landon checked his e-mail and then hurried down for breakfast.

"Hey, Mom, do you think I can go to a movie tonight with some friends?"

"Only if your chores are done," replied his mom.

At lunchtime, Landon swiped his card in the lunch machine, but it showed that he had already eaten lunch today. He went to class to take his math test, but found his name and score already recorded on the computer. He had not gotten a good grade.

"How can this be?" he asked.

After school, he stopped by the movie theater to pick up a reserved ticket to the latest alien movie—but the lady said that a ticket had already been purchased in his name. Something was wrong! Landon hurried home to see what was going on. He read an e-mail from his own computer. It read, "Landon, I am tired of doing the work in your life, and I have decided to do the fun things in your life as well. Signed, Your Computer."

"What?" asked Landon. "I've got to reprogram this thing, and quickly. I can do my own chores. Who needs a computer to do that?" Landon spent the next two hours reprogramming his computer and fell exhausted on his bed. He wondered if the computer had already slept for him that night. He hoped not.

## STORY QUESTIONS

**1.** Which of the following could be a title for this story?

   a. "The Case of the Missing Computer"

   b. "The Day My Computer Crashed"

   c. "Invasion of the Computer"

   d. "The Computer Clicks"

**2.** What is the meaning of the word *swiped* as used in the story?

   a. run through      c. interrogate

   b. open up      d. align

**3.** What sentence in this story indicates that it is a fantasy story?

   a. Landon spent the next two hours reprogramming his computer.

   b. He wondered if the computer had already slept for him that night.

   c. He had not gotten a good grade.

   d. Landon started up his computer like he did every day.

# FLY AWAY HOME

The Jenson family planned a summer vacation each year that was out of this world. This summer they decided to make their first trip in their new machine. That's right—Mr. Jensen had invented the first car/spacecraft combination ever. His machine could fly or drive at the flip of a switch. The hours in a car were shortened; and if they wanted to explore, they just went back to car mode.

The Jensons were excited to try out the machine. Their trip to the Grand Canyon was sure to be a hit. The first day of travel was smooth. They reached Flagstaff, Arizona with plenty of time to hit the hot tub.

The next morning, they began their drive to the Grand Canyon. As they boarded, Mr. Jenson flipped the switch to fly so that they could hover over the Grand Canyon and check out the beautiful site. They hovered in the air. All of a sudden, there was a crackling sound and the car immediately began its descent. It descended all the way down to the bottom of the canyon at record speed. The car came to a screeching halt.

"Is everyone okay?" asked Mr. Jenson. No one said a word. They climbed out of the machine. They were happy to be on solid ground again.

"Come on! Isn't anyone going to get back in the car with me?"

"No, thanks," the other Jensons replied. "We'll wait for the next burro to come along."

## STORY QUESTIONS

1. Which words best describe Mr. Jenson in the story?
   a. creative, outgoing, confident
   b. timid, shy, new
   c. timid, obnoxious, scared
   d. stuck up, timid, excited

2. Which of the following statements is <u>not</u> part of the story?
   a. The family members were afraid to get back in Mr. Jenson's machine.
   b. Mr. Jenson is upset with his family for leaving him.
   c. Mr. Jenson is an inventor.
   d. Mr. Jenson's family is supportive at first.

3. What is the problem in the story?
   a. Mr. Jenson is feeling sorry for himself.
   b. The machine didn't work as planned.
   c. None of the family members trust Mr. Jenson.
   d. Mr. Jenson has not completed his machine.

# MAKE A WISH

Nora sat by the well and washed her dishes. Today had been a very hot day. She scooped an extra bucket of water from the well to quench her thirst. As she lowered the bucket again, she happened to notice a small cup resting on a rock just outside the well. When she brought the water up again, she picked up the cup and set it by her stack of dishes.

Nora used the water to wash the dishes. As she rubbed the small cup, a cloud of smoke and a genie appeared. Nora was stunned. She did not know whether to run or stay.

"Do not be afraid," said the genie. "I am the genie of the cup. I will grant you three wishes."

"Three wishes?" asked Nora in disbelief.

"Three wishes, but that is all—so choose your wishes wisely."

Nora's first wish was to have all the toys she ever wanted. Her wish was granted. But after five minutes of being with all the toys, she was ready to have some peace. Each toy made its own noise, and Nora could hardly hear herself think.

Her second wish was to have all of her favorite foods. Nora realized this, too, was a foolish wish because she got so full that she felt sick.

She wised up for her final wish and stated, "I wish to give my wish to someone else."

"Wise choice," said the genie, who then disappeared inside the cup.

## STORY QUESTIONS

1. What did Nora learn from this experience?
   a. Her life needed a lot of changes.
   b. She realized she needed to be better prepared to make a wish.
   c. She was content with what she already had.
   d. She knew she could not trust the genie.

2. What can you learn about Nora from reading this passage?
   a. She likes to make wishes.
   b. She wishes the genie was gone.
   c. She lives a fantasy life.
   d. She is able to learn from her mistakes.

3. Which of the following would also make a good title for this story?
   a. "The Three Wishes"           c. "Lessons for the Cup"
   b. "The Genie and the Lamp"      d. "Mr. Genie"

# *THE LEGEND*

The bugle blew to signal that it was time to get up. Byron rolled over in his sleeping bag. Today was the day they could earn their swimming badge; but after the 10-mile hike yesterday, Byron wondered if he had it in him. Byron grabbed his water shoes and left.

As the boys lined up, there was talk about the legendary monster that lived in the lake. It had been a rumor for years. No one dared admit that he believed in the lake monster.

The whistle blew for the first set of boys to dive in. Byron watched from the shore. Before long, it was time for him to swim. He readied himself and dove in at the sound of the whistle.

He was swimming gracefully across the water, but he was not at the front. He knew he'd have to really push himself to make the cut. Just then, he felt a push on his back. It felt like a tail of sorts. Spectators from the shore were hollering about the monster on Byron's back. Byron didn't know what to think, so he just kept swimming. He managed to take the lead and promptly set the camp record.

The crowd went wild. He had never gone that fast before in his life. Was it really the tail of the monster? He knew he had felt something scaly on his back. But was it really the monster? Byron shrugged his shoulders and headed towards the showers.

## STORY QUESTIONS

*1.* Which sentence shows that Byron might believe in the lake monster?

    a. The crowd had seen the monster.

    b. He knew he had felt something scaly on his back.

    c. Bryon believed in the monster before he entered the race.

    d. The camp counselor told Byron about the monster.

*2.* What is the meaning of the word *promptly* as used in the story?

    a. honestly

    b. with precision

    c. quickly

    d. carefully

*3.* Which of the following statements did <u>not</u> happen in the story?

    a. Byron saw the lake monster.

    b. The crowd said they saw the monster on Byron's back.

    c. Some people in the camp believed in the monster.

    d. The lake monster was a rumor for years.

Name _____    Date _____

# THE TOE HAIR

Princess Jane hated to see her brother so sick. She had to do something! She had read in a book about potions and was determined to make one. One potion guaranteed to make the sick well. The only problem was that in order to make the potion complete, she needed a hair from a witch's toe.

The witch of the forest lived in the deserted castle. Princess Jane would sneak in at night. That evening, she set out early so that she would have plenty of time to get there. In her mind, she went through all the problems she might encounter. There was no doubt she was nervous. She had heard wild stories about the witch.

That night she snuck up to the bedroom of the witch and peered over the bed. She could see her toe sticking out from underneath the covers. She gently raised herself up and pulled out her tweezers. She snapped a hair and pulled pack.

Just then, the witch sat up and screamed, "What are you doing?"

Jane was speechless. She didn't know what to say, so she responded, "Giving you a pedicure."

"Well, enough of that. I made an appointment for a massage, not a pedicure. Get up here and give me a back rub."

And so Jane did. There was a twinkle in her eye as she slipped the toe hair into her purse. "Hang in there, brother," she thought. Her luck couldn't have been better.

## STORY QUESTIONS

*1.* What is the problem in this story?
   a. The witch wakes up.
   b. Princess Jane's brother is sick, and she wants to help.
   c. The witch screams at Jane.
   d. Princess Jane had to give the witch a back rub.

*2.* What attribute does Princess Jane display in this story?
   a. anger
   b. courage
   c. selfishness
   d. forgiveness

*3.* Which of the following events happened in the story?
   a. The witch is known for her torture treatments.
   b. Princess Jane has lunch with the witch.
   c. The witch knows who Princess Jane is.
   d. The witch reacts differently than Princess Jane thought she would.

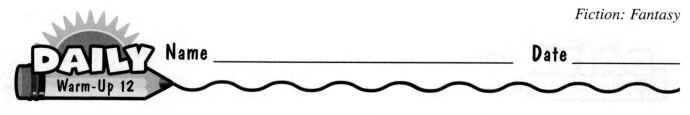

Name _____     Date _____

# OPEN UP

Christine and Ella were all decked out in their Halloween costumes.  They were excited for the big night.  They said goodbye to their parents and set out to have some fun.  They stopped at all of the homes they wanted to for trick-or-treating and then went around to see if they could find any of their friends.

They met up with some girls who went to their school.  There was talk that night that Jed Barrow was dressed up like Frankenstein and was pretty convincing.  The night wore on, and the girls laughed and scared little kids walking by.  It was starting to get late, and Christine and Ella decided that they should be heading home.  They said goodbye to their friends and headed down the next street.  This street was quiet for some reason, and it made them nervous.  They quickened their pace a bit.  Just then, they saw someone lurking around the corner who looked like Frankenstein.

Christine let out a scream and began running.  Ella was close behind.  Frankenstein was yelling and calling after them.  They could barely stay two feet ahead of him.  They finally reached Ella's house and ran inside.  They slammed the door shut just in the nick of time.

But Frankenstein did not go away.  He kept pounding on the door, saying, "Open up!"  Frankenstein didn't leave until Ella's dad came home and hollered for him to leave.  Ella and Christine began to wonder if this Frankenstein was their friend Jed or if it was the real deal.  At school, Jed denied it.  It became their favorite story to share at all their slumber parties.

## STORY QUESTIONS

*1.* Ella and Christine shared a . . .

　　a. costume.

　　b. favorite treat.

　　c. funny joke.

　　d. scary evening.

*2.* What evidence is there to show that this wasn't a pretend Frankenstein?

　　a. Jed mentioned the experience at school.

　　b. Jed denied that it had been him.

　　c. Jed revealed himself to the girls.

　　d. The girls don't believe in monsters.

*3.* The best way to find the answer to the previous question is to . . .

　　a. reread the entire passage.

　　b. skim the passage and determine the main idea.

　　c. reread the ending and search for clues.

　　d. guess.

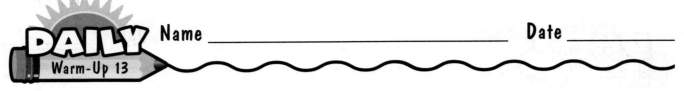

# GROCERY SHOPPING

Emma and Ed were twins. They had been asked to stop by the grocery store on their way home from school. The twins met up after school and headed for the store.

Emma pulled the list out of her backpack.

"Bread, milk, apples . . . It's all here," said Emma.

"Does it say anything about cereal?" asked Ed.

"Of course, but it doesn't say the kind. I guess that means you get to pick it out," said Emma.

"Yes!" replied Ed.

Ed made his way to the cereal aisle. He loved to pick out the cereal. He walked down the aisle until he found his cereal. He reached up on the high shelf to pull down a box. But instead of the box, he touched something else! He looked up to see a hand where the box was. The hand reached down and pulled Ed up in the air. He was dangling from the cereal shelf.

"Help!" he called. There was no response. "Help!" he tried again. This time he could see Emma coming down the aisle. Emma saw Ed dangling and reached up to pull him down.

"Ed! What are you doing? I can't take you anywhere," said Emma.

Ed was stunned. He tried to catch his breath. Emma reached down, picked up a box of cereal, and threw it in the cart. Ed couldn't move, so Emma grabbed his hand and pulled him away. Ed glanced back at the aisle. He could see the hand waving at him.

## STORY QUESTIONS

1. Which of the following would make a good title for the story?
   a. "Up, Up, and Away"
   b. "The Hand in the Store"
   c. "Give Him a Hand"
   d. "Grocery Shopping with Emma"

2. Does Emma understand what happened to Ed?
   a. No. She thinks that Ed is playing around.
   b. Yes, and she is tired of him messing around.
   c. Yes. She could see it happening from the next aisle over.
   d. No, but the store owner told her what was going on.

3. Which sentence from the story helps you answer the previous question?
   a. Ed glanced back at the aisle.
   b. Ed was stunned.
   c. Emma saw Ed dangling and reached up to pull him down.
   d. "Ed! What are you doing? I can't take you anywhere," said Emma.

Name _____     Date _____

# TOUCH AND GO

Brett had been planning a fishing trip for a very long time.  He loaded his gear and hiked down to the river.  He set up his pole and leaned back against a rock.  Just then, he felt a tug on his line like he had never felt before.  He began reeling his line in and pulled as hard as he could.  Out popped a fish at the end of his line.  It was a big one!  Brett continued to reel it in.  He cut the line and took the fishhook out of the mouth of the fish.  As he set it in a pail of water, the fish began to talk!

"Hey, Brett," said the fish, "you sure caught a good one, didn't you?"

"What?" asked Brett in an astonished voice.  "You can talk?"

"I can talk," said the fish.  "I can even tell your future."

"You can?" asked Brett, still stunned.

"I can," said the fish.  "You are going to have a science test tomorrow and you haven't studied for it."

"Wow," said Brett as he contemplated what it might be like to have a fish that could talk and tell his future.

"I also know that you didn't make your bed this morning, and you will be served broccoli tonight at dinner," stated the fish.

At this point, Brett realized that he didn't really need this talking fish and threw him back into the river.  He gathered his pole and headed home.  He'd had enough fishing for the day.

## STORY QUESTIONS

1. Which word best describes Brett in the story?
   a. surprised
   b. lazy
   c. timid
   d. obtuse

2. Which of the following statements is <u>not</u> accurate?
   a. The fish was calling Brett by his name.
   b. Brett realized that he didn't want this fish.
   c. Brett caught a fish that could talk.
   d. The fish was able to share good news about Brett's future.

3. What is the problem in the story?
   a. Brett catches a fish that can foresee his future and realizes it's not a good thing.
   b. Brett is worried that he hasn't studied for his science test yet.
   c. Brett had to leave early and wasn't able to catch very many fish.
   d. Brett fears for his life because of the talking fish.

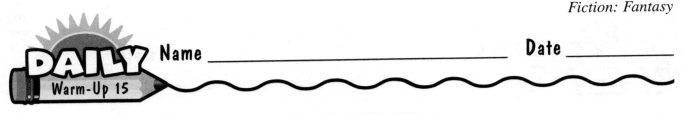

Name _____ Date _____

# ROUND 'EM UP

Cameron loved to ride his horse, Sandy, with the cowboys on the ranch. This year, they were rounding up the cows at the north end of the ranch. The terrain there was steep and rugged. They found the cows up against the side of Bluff Mountain. Things went well, and the cows seemed to respond well to their coaxing. But just then, a cow bolted and headed in the opposite direction. Cameron swerved off to the right to try to get her.

It wasn't an easy task. The cow ran faster and faster. Cameron glanced down just in time to realize that he was about to run out of ground. The cow veered sharply to the left, and Cameron jerked back on the reins. It was too late. He knew he was going off the cliff, and there was nothing he could do about it.

Instead of falling, they continued sailing through the air. They kept going through the air until they reached the other side. Cameron was stunned. How did they do that? He couldn't believe what had just happened. He climbed down to look at Sandy. She had a gleam in her eye. Cameron made his way back to the ranch house to meet up with the group.

"How did you fair?" asked Cameron's dad.

"Let's just say that we sailed through," said Cameron, still in shock.

"I knew you could do it, Cameron," said his dad. Cameron rode Sandy back to stable. He couldn't wait to get out of the saddle.

## STORY QUESTIONS

1. What does *terrain* mean as used in this story?
   a. aligned
   b. vertical
   c. cliff
   d. land

2. Which sentence below resolves the problem in the story?
   a. Cameron jerked back on the reins.
   b. Instead of falling, they continued sailing through the air.
   c. Cameron skirted off to the right to try and get her.
   d. He climbed down to look at Sandy.

3. What is another good title for this story passage?
   a. "Cameron's Amazing Ride"
   b. "Sailing the Seas"
   c. "Cowboys and Indians"
   d. "Rounding Up Cattle Techniques"

# ANSWER KEY

# Answer Key

## Nonfiction Passages
## Animals

**Page 9  Ladybugs**
1. b
2. d
3. She will soon marry.
4. c

**Page 10  The Panda Bear**
1. b
2. a
3. c
4. d

**Page 11  Killer Whales**
1. d
2. b
3. c
4. d

**Page 12  The Sloth**
1. c
2. b
3. a
4. b

**Page 13  The Rattlesnake**
1. d
2. b
3. c
4. a

**Page 14  The Praying Mantis**
1. a
2. b
3. d
4. c

**Page 15  The Bison**
1. c
2. b
3. d
4. a

**Page 16  Flamingos**
1. d
2. b
3. c

**Page 17  The Giraffe**
1. b
2. a
3. c

**Page 18  The Monarch Butterfly**
1. b
2. c
3. d

**Page 19  Desert Tortoise**
1. a
2. c
3. d
4. b

**Page 20  Clown Fish**
1. a
2. d
3. b

**Page 21  The Mountain Lion**
1. a
2. c
3. c
4. b

**Page 22  Gecko Lizards**
1. b
2. a
3. d
4. b

**Page 23  The Jellyfish**
1. c
2. d
3. c
4. a

**Page 24  The Wombat**
1. c
2. c
3. b
4. c

## Biography

**Page 25  Walt Disney**
1. d
2. c
3. b
4. a

**Page 26  Helen Keller**
1. c
2. b
3. c

**Page 27  Babe Ruth**
1. c
2. b
3. d

**Page 28  Henry Ford**
1. c
2. a
3. b
4. d

**Page 29  Laura Ingalls Wilder**
1. a
2. c
3. a
4. d

**Page 30  Claude Monet**
1. b
2. c
3. b
4. c

**Page 31  Dr. Seuss**
1. c
2. a
3. d
4. a

**Page 32  John Glenn**
1. b
2. c
3. d

**Page 33  Abigail Adams**
1. b
2. a
3. d
4. c

**Page 34  Elvis Presley**
1. b
2. c
3. d
4. c

**Page 35  Eleanor Roosevelt**
1. c
2. d
3. a
4. b

**Page 36  Alexander Graham Bell**
1. b
2. c
3. a
4. c

**Page 37  John F. Kennedy**
1. c
2. b
3. d
4. b

**Page 38  Charles Lindbergh**
1. c
2. d
3. a
4. b

**Page 39  Oprah Winfrey**
1. c
2. a
3. c
4. b

**Page 40  Jesse Owens**
1. b
2. c
3. c
4. d

## American History

**Page 41  Boston Tea Party**
1. c
2. d
3. c
4. c

**Page 42  Segregation**
1. a
2. c
3. d
4. d

**Page 43  Pearl Harbor**
1. c
2. a
3. b
4. d

**Page 44  Man on the Moon**
1. c
2. b
3. b
4. a

**Page 45  The Gettysburg Address**
1. c
2. a
3. d
4. c

**Page 46  The Star-Spangled Banner**
1. b
2. b
3. c
4. d

**Page 47  The New England Colonies**
1. c
2. d
3. a

**Page 48  Ellis Island**
1. d
2. c
3. c

**Page 49  Alaska Becomes a State**
1. c
2. d
3. a
4. b

**Page 50  Westward, Ho!**
1. c
2. d
3. a
4. b

**Page 51  Southern Plantations**
1. d
2. d
3. c
4. c

**Page 52  Women's Rights**
1. d
2. b
3. a

**Page 53  The Dust Bowl**
1. b
2. b
3. d

**Page 54  Leisure Time in America**
1. a
2. d
3. c
4. b

**Page 55  I Have a Dream**
1. b
2. b
3. c

# Science

**Page 56  Jupiter**
1. a
2. d
3. d
4. b

**Page 57  The Central Nervous System**
1. b
2. d
3. d

**Page 58  Mercury**
1. c
2. b
3. a
4. c

**Page 59  Uranus**
1. b
2. c
3. a
4. d

**Page 60  Earth's Atmosphere**
1. b
2. c
3. a

**Page 61  Earthquakes**
1. c
2. a
3. c

**Page 62  Amphibians**
1. b
2. b
3. a
4. c

**Page 63  The Ear**
1. c
2. d
3. c

**Page 64  Insects**
1. b
2. d
3. c
4. b

**Page 65  The Circulatory System**
1. c
2. d
3. d
4. a

**Page 66  The Muscular System**
1. a
2. c
3. b
4. d

**Page 67  Tornadoes**
1. b
2. a
3. b
4. c

**Page 68  Constellations**
1. a
2. b
3. d
4. c

**Page 69  Venus**
1. d
2. a
3. c
4. b

**Page 70  Asteroid Belt**
1. c
2. a
3. a
4. d

**Page 71  The Oceans**
1. c
2. d
3. c
4. c

# Current Events

**Page 72  Childhood Obesity**
1. c
2. a
3. d

# Answer Key

**Page 96  Housework**
1. It meant that she needed to do her fair share of the work.
2. b
3. c

**Page 97  Princess Problems**
1. d
2. a
3. a

**Page 98  Funny Frieda**
1. d
2. d
3. c
4. a

**Page 99  Early to Rise**
1. c
2. d
3. b

**Page 100  Practicing Patience**
1. d
2. a
3. b

**Page 101  Scrambled Eggs**
1. c
2. a
3. d

**Page 102  In Need**
1. b
2. c
3. c

**Page 103  Perfection**
1. c
2. a

3. They learned that if you practice hard enough, you can show improvement—even great improvement.

**Page 104  Surprising Twist**
1. c
2. c
3. c

# Historical Fiction

**Page 105  Civil Love**
1. b
2. a
3. c
4. c

**Page 106  Welcome Home**
1. d
2. d
3. b

**Page 107  You're Fired**
1. d
2. d
3. d

**Page 108  Baby Doll**
1. Grace had a conversation about the doll with the man at the store.
2. b
3. c

**Page 109  The Gettysburg Address**
1. c
2. a
3. d

**Page 110  Maren's Wish**
1. b
2. b

3. a

**Page 111  The Uniform**
1. d
2. b
3. b

**Page 112  Refuge from the Storm**
1. b
2. a
3. b

**Page 113  Shot Heard Around the World**
1. a
2. b
3. b

**Page 114  Blast Off!**
1. a
2. c
3. c

**Page 115  Being Needled**
1. c
2. d
3. b

**Page 116  Over the Top**
1. b
2. d
3. a

**Page 117  Sacrifice Brings Blessings**
1. d
2. b
3. b

**Page 118  Sick of It**
1. d
2. c
3. a

**Page 119  Out of the Dust**
1. c
2. d
3. d

## Contemporary Realistic Fiction

**Page 120  Spelling Bee**
1. c
2. d
3. a

**Page 121  Bake-Sale Blues**
1. d
2. b
3. a

**Page 122  Overboard!**
1. d
2. c
3. b

**Page 123  Artistic Talent**
1. d
2. d
3. b
4. c

**Page 124  The Field Trip**
1. b
2. a
3. b

**Page 125  A Sudsy Day**
1. b
2. d
3. b

**Page 126  The Field Day**
1. a
2. d
3. d

**Page 127  Family Reunion**
1. a
2. b
3. d

**Page 128  Haunted Halloween**
1. a
2. b
3. c

**Page 129  Friends in the Morning**
1. c
2. c
3. b

**Page 130  The Attack at Midnight**
1. b
2. c
3. a

**Page 131  Faded Memories**
1. b
2. c
3. b

**Page 132  Mystery Solved**
1. b
2. d
3. a

**Page 133  My Dog Ate It**
1. a
2. b
3. d

**Page 134  Ski Buddies**
1. c
2. a
3. c

**Page 135  I Spy!**
1. c
2. b
3. d
4. b

## Mystery/Suspense/ Adventure

**Page 136  The Cave**
1. b
2. c
3. a

**Page 137  Ironing Board Surfing**
1. c
2. b
3. c

**Page 138  April Fool's Day**
1. c
2. a
3. b

**Page 139  The Treasure**
1. c
2. b
3. b

**Page 140  The Chess Champion**
1. a
2. b
3. d

**Page 141  Here Comes the Dog!**
1. c
2. b
3. c

# Answer Key

**Page 142   The Peeping Tom**
1. d
2. b
3. a

**Page 143   The Missing Shoe**
1. c
2. a
3. d

**Page 144   The Mysterious Mail**
1. c
2. d
3. a

**Page 145   The Stolen Bike**
1. a
2. d
3. d

**Page 146   Wild Things in the Closet**
1. a
2. d
3. c
4. d

**Page 147   The Secret Friend**
1. b
2. c
3. b

**Page 148   S.O.S.**
1. a
2. c
3. d

**Page 149   Puppy Love**
1. d
2. a
3. b
4. c

**Page 150   Alarming Discovery**
1. c
2. d
3. d

**Page 151   Racing for Friendship**
1. b
2. b
3. c

## Fantasy

**Page 152   The Disappearing Cat**
1. a
2. c
3. c
4. a

**Page 153   Will Power**
1. c
2. a
3. d

**Page 154   Volleyball Venue**
1. a
2. d
3. c

**Page 155   Martian Madness**
1. b
2. c
3. d

**Page 156   The Quest**
1. c
2. b
3. c

**Page 157   Football Practice**
1. c
2. b
3. b

**Page 158   Computer Virus**
1. c
2. a
3. b

**Page 159   Fly Away Home**
1. a
2. b
3. b

**Page 160   Make a Wish**
1. c
2. d
3. a

**Page 161   The Legend**
1. b
2. c
3. a

**Page 162   The Toe Hair**
1. b
2. b
3. d

**Page 163   Open Up**
1. d
2. b
3. c

**Page 164   Grocery Shopping**
1. b
2. a
3. d

**Page 165   Touch and Go**
1. a
2. d
3. a

**Page 166   Round 'Em Up**
1. d
2. b
3. a

# Leveling Chart

NONFICTION ▲ = below grade level ● = at grade level ■ = above grade level

| Animals | | Biography | | American History | | Science | | Current Events | |
|---|---|---|---|---|---|---|---|---|---|
| Page 9 | ● | Page 25 | ■ | Page 41 | ● | Page 56 | ■ | Page 72 | ■ |
| Page 10 | ● | Page 26 | ● | Page 42 | ● | Page 57 | ● | Page 73 | ● |
| Page 11 | ● | Page 27 | ● | Page 43 | ■ | Page 58 | ■ | Page 74 | ■ |
| Page 12 | ▲ | Page 28 | ■ | Page 44 | ▲ | Page 59 | ■ | Page 75 | ■ |
| Page 13 | ■ | Page 29 | ■ | Page 45 | ■ | Page 60 | ■ | Page 76 | ■ |
| Page 14 | ● | Page 30 | ● | Page 46 | ● | Page 61 | ● | Page 77 | ■ |
| Page 15 | ● | Page 31 | ● | Page 47 | ■ | Page 62 | ● | Page 78 | ● |
| Page 16 | ● | Page 32 | ■ | Page 48 | ■ | Page 63 | ▲ | Page 79 | ● |
| Page 17 | ● | Page 33 | ■ | Page 49 | ■ | Page 64 | ■ | Page 80 | |
| Page 18 | ■ | Page 34 | ● | Page 50 | ■ | Page 65 | ● | Page 81 | ■ |
| Page 19 | ■ | Page 35 | ■ | Page 51 | ▲ | Page 66 | ● | Page 82 | ■ |
| Page 20 | ▲ | Page 36 | ● | Page 52 | ● | Page 67 | ● | Page 83 | ■ |
| Page 21 | ● | Page 37 | ● | Page 53 | ● | Page 68 | ▲ | Page 84 | ■ |
| Page 22 | ● | Page 38 | ● | Page 54 | ■ | Page 69 | ● | Page 85 | ■ |
| Page 23 | ■ | Page 39 | ■ | Page 55 | ■ | Page 70 | ■ | Page 86 | ■ |
| Page 24 | ● | Page 40 | ■ | | | Page 71 | ● | | |

FICTION ▲ = below grade level ● = at grade level ■ = above grade level

| Fairy Tales/Folklore | | Historical Fiction | | Contemporary Realistic Fiction | | Mystery/Suspense/Adventure | | Fantasy | |
|---|---|---|---|---|---|---|---|---|---|
| Page 89 | ▲ | Page 105 | ● | Page 120 | ▲ | Page 136 | ▲ | Page 152 | ▲ |
| Page 90 | ● | Page 106 | ▲ | Page 121 | ▲ | Page 137 | ● | Page 153 | ▲ |
| Page 91 | ● | Page 107 | ▲ | Page 122 | ▲ | Page 138 | ● | Page 154 | ● |
| Page 92 | ▲ | Page 108 | ▲ | Page 123 | ● | Page 139 | ● | Page 155 | ● |
| Page 93 | ● | Page 109 | ● | Page 124 | ● | Page 140 | ● | Page 156 | ● |
| Page 94 | ▲ | Page 110 | ▲ | Page 125 | ● | Page 141 | ▲ | Page 157 | ▲ |
| Page 95 | ▲ | Page 111 | ▲ | Page 126 | ● | Page 142 | ● | Page 158 | ● |
| Page 96 | ● | Page 112 | ▲ | Page 127 | ▲ | Page 143 | ▲ | Page 159 | ● |
| Page 97 | ▲ | Page 113 | ● | Page 128 | ● | Page 144 | ● | Page 160 | ▲ |
| Page 98 | ▲ | Page 114 | ● | Page 129 | ▲ | Page 145 | ▲ | Page 161 | ▲ |
| Page 99 | ▲ | Page 115 | ● | Page 130 | ● | Page 146 | ▲ | Page 162 | ▲ |
| Page 100 | ● | Page 116 | ▲ | Page 131 | ▲ | Page 147 | ▲ | Page 163 | ● |
| Page 101 | ● | Page 117 | ▲ | Page 132 | ▲ | Page 148 | ▲ | Page 164 | ▲ |
| Page 102 | ▲ | Page 118 | ● | Page 133 | ● | Page 149 | ▲ | Page 165 | ▲ |
| Page 103 | ● | Page 119 | ● | Page 134 | ▲ | Page 150 | ● | Page 166 | ▲ |
| Page 104 | ▲ | | | Page 135 | ▲ | Page 151 | ▲ | | |

# Congratulations to

_____

# for completing

_____

_____

_____
*Signature*

_____
*Date*

**Editor**
Mary S. Jones, M.A.

**Managing Editor**
Karen J. Goldfluss, M.S. Ed.

**Cover Artist**
Brenda DiAntonis

**Art Production Manager**
Kevin Barnes

**Art Coordinator**
Renée Christine Yates

**Imaging**
James Edward Grace
Ricardo Martinez

**Publisher**
Mary D. Smith, M.S. Ed.

# DAILY WARM-UPS
## Reading
### GRADE 4

- Over 150 nonfiction and fiction passages
- Follow-up questions for each passage target essential comprehension skills.
- Ideal for test preparation!

Reading

**Author**

*Sarah Kartchner Clark, M.A.*

Teacher Created Resources

**Teacher Created Resources, Inc.**
6421 Industry Way
Westminster, CA 92683
www.teachercreated.com
**ISBN-1-4206-3490-9**
©2006 Teacher Created Resources, Inc.
Made in U.S.A.

# Table of Contents

Ladybugs—The Panda Bear—Killer Whales—The Sloth—The Rattlesnake—
The Praying Mantis—The Bison—Flamingos—The Giraffe—The Monarch
Butterfly—Desert Tortoise—Clown Fish—The Mountain Lion—Gecko
Lizards—The Jellyfish—The Wombat

Walt Disney—Helen Keller—Babe Ruth—Henry Ford—Laura Ingalls
Wilder—Claude Monet—Dr. Seuss—John Glenn—Abigail Adams—Elvis
Presley—Eleanor Roosevelt—Alexander Graham Bell—John F. Kennedy—
Charles Lindbergh—Oprah Winfrey—Jesse Owens

Boston Tea Party—Segregation—Pearl Harbor—Man on the Moon—The
Gettysburg Address—The Star-Spangled Banner—The New England
Colonies—Ellis Island—Alaska Becomes a State—Westward, Ho!—Southern
Plantations—Women's Rights—The Dust Bowl—Leisure Time in America—
I Have a Dream

Jupiter—The Central Nervous System—Mercury—Uranus—Earth's
Atmosphere—Earthquakes—Amphibians—The Ear—Insects—The
Circulatory System—The Muscular System—Tornadoes—Constellations—
Venus—The Asteroid Belt—The Oceans

Childhood Obesity—Littering—Teacher Selection—Character Education—
Too Much TV!—School Uniforms—Enough Sleep—Amount of Homework—
Heavy Backpacks—Cell Phones—School Lunch Menu—Quality of
Children's Movies—Extracurricular Activities—Discipline at School—Drug-
Prevention Programs